Women of Achievement

Susan B. Anthony

Women of Achievement

Susan B. Anthony

Hillary Rodham Clinton

Marie Curie

Ellen DeGeneres

Nancy Pelosi

Rachael Ray

Eleanor Roosevelt

Martha Stewart

Women of Achievement

Susan B. Anthony

ACTIVIST

Anne M. Todd

CHELSEA HOUSE
PUBLISHERS
An imprint of Infobase Publishing

SUSAN B. ANTHONY

Chelsea House
An imprint of Infobase Publishing
132 West 31st Street
New York NY 10001

Library of Congress Cataloging-in-Publication Data
Todd, Anne M.
  Susan B. Anthony : Activist /Anne M. Todd.
    p. cm. — (Women of achievement)
  Includes bibliographical references and index.
  ISBN 978-1-60413-087-4 (hardcover : acid-free paper) 1. Anthony, Susan B.
(Susan Brownell), 1820-1906. 2. Feminists—United States—Biography.
3. Suffragists—United States—Biography. 4. Women's rights—United States—
History. 5. Women—Suffrage—United States—History. I. Title. II. Series.
  HQ1413.A55T63 2009
  324.6'23092—dc22
  [B]   2008034641

Chelsea House books are available at special discounts when purchased in bulk quantities for businesses, associations, institutions, or sales promotions. Please call our Special Sales Department in New York at (212) 967-8800 or (800) 322-8755.

You can find Chelsea House on the World Wide Web at http://www.chelseahouse.com

Series design by Erik Lindstrom
Cover design by Ben Peterson

Printed in the United States of America

Bang FOF 10 9 8 7 6 5 4 3 2 1

This book is printed on acid-free paper.

All links and Web addresses were checked and verified to be correct at the time of publication. Because of the dynamic nature of the Web, some addresses and links may have changed since publication and may no longer be valid.

CONTENTS

1   Arrested for Voting   7

2   A Quaker Upbringing   13

3   The Power of Reform   26

4   Breaking Down Fences   43

5   The American Civil War and Its Aftermath   55

6   A Tower of Strength   73

7   A New Generation of Women   93

8   A Life Gone, but Not Forgotten   108

Chronology   113

Notes   116

Bibliography   121

Further Resources   122

Picture Credits   123

Index   124

About the Author   128

7

Arrested
for Voting

"**F**riends and Fellow-citizens: I stand before you to-night, under indictment for the alleged crime of having voted at the last Presidential election, without having a lawful right to vote. It shall be my work this evening to prove to you that in thus voting, I not only committed no crime, but, instead, simply exercised my citizen's right, guaranteed to me and all United States citizens by the National Constitution, beyond the power of any State to deny."[1]

So began Susan B. Anthony's speech, entitled "Is It a Crime for a Citizen of the United States to Vote?" At that time in American history, in 1872, it was illegal for a woman to cast a ballot during an election in the United States. Anthony had already spent much of her life trying to change that law. She believed that, as citizens of the

United States, women had the same rights as men. The U.S. government did not share her belief. Authorities arrested Anthony for an illegal vote in a federal election in November 1872.

Prior to the vote and her arrest, Anthony had managed to sway election officials in Rochester, New York, to allow her (and 15 other women—including Anthony's three sisters, Guelma, Hannah, and Mary) to register to vote. Anthony told the election officials that she was claiming their right to vote not under the Constitution of the State of New York, but rather under the Fourteenth Amendment of the Constitution of the United States. The Fourteenth Amendment, in part, says that all people born in the United States are citizens of the United States and are entitled to the privileges of citizenship; Anthony believed that those privileges included voting. After discussion, the officials allowed the women to register.

Four days later, Anthony cast the only presidential ballot she would make in her lifetime: She voted for Republican Ulysses S. Grant. Anthony described her decision to vote this way: "I voted in the State of New York in 1872 under the construction of [the Fourteenth and Fifteenth] amendments, which we felt to be the true one, that all persons born in the United States, or any State thereof, and under the jurisdiction of the United States, were citizens, and entitled to equality of rights, and that no State could deprive them of their equality of rights."[2]

A few weeks later, on Thanksgiving Day, a U.S. marshal came to Anthony's red brick home, located on Madison Street in Rochester, New York, and arrested her. Her bail was set at $1,000. Anthony's attorney paid the bail money, and Anthony immediately set out to deliver

AMENDING THE UNITED STATES CONSTITUTION

Amending the United States Constitution is not easy. In fact, as of 2008, the Constitution had only 27 amendments. (The Fourteenth Amendment, which Susan B. Anthony believed gave her the right to vote, was ratified in 1868.) An amendment goes through four steps to become part of the Constitution:

1. First, Congress must agree upon the wording of an amendment, which means that a two-thirds vote from both houses—the House of Representatives and the Senate—must agree on the proposed amendment. The president of the United States is not involved in approving a proposed amendment.

2. Once Congress has passed a proposed amendment, it is sent to the National Archives. Someone from the National Archives sends a copy of the proposed amendment to the governor of each state. Along with the proposed copy is a form that is filled out if the state decides to ratify (or approve) the amendment.

3. Each state legislature decides whether it agrees with the amendment. States may not make any changes in the language of the proposed amendment. A vote in favor of ratification means that the state agrees with the amendment and wants to see it added to the Constitution.

4. In order for a proposed amendment to take effect, three-fourths of the states must ratify the amendment. The Office of the Federal Register at the National Archives keeps the official count.

Women's rights activist Susan B. Anthony stands on the porch of her family's home at 17 Madison Street in Rochester, New York, in the 1870s. U.S. marshals came to the home in November 1872 to arrest her for voting in the presidential election. It was the only presidential election in which Anthony would ever participate.

her speech, "Is It a Crime for a Citizen of the United States to Vote?" She did so for the next three weeks, traveling to 29 of the towns and villages in Monroe County and 21 towns in Ontario County. In each town, people gathered to hear Anthony speak out about the injustice of her arrest and why women should have voting rights.

JUSTICE ISN'T SERVED

The following summer, on June 17, 1873, Anthony's trial began at the U.S. Circuit Court in Canandaigua, New York. Yet Judge Ward Hunt had made his decision about the case long before setting foot in the courtroom. Hunt instructed the 12 male jurors to find Susan B. Anthony guilty. He said to them, "The question, gentlemen of the jury … is wholly a question or questions of law, and I have decided as a question of law, in the first place, that under the Fourteenth Amendment, which Miss Anthony claims protects her, she was not protected in a right to vote. And I have decided also that her belief and the advice which she took do not protect her in the act which she committed. If I am right in this, the result must be a verdict on your part of guilty, and I therefore direct that you find a verdict of guilty."[3] The jury obliged. When Anthony had earlier tried to testify in her own defense, Hunt had barred her from taking the stand.

After the verdict, Anthony was finally allowed to speak, but Judge Hunt frequently interrupted her and cut her off, insisting that "the court cannot allow the prisoner to go on."[4] When he later told Anthony that she had been tried according to the established forms of law, she responded, "Yes, your honor, but by forms of law all made by men, interpreted by men, administered by men, in favor of men, and against women; and hence, your honor's ordered verdict of guilty, against a United States citizen for the exercise of 'that citizen's right to vote,' simply because that citizen was a woman and not a man."[5]

Anthony's words fell to deaf ears. Judge Hunt ordered Susan B. Anthony to pay a $100 fine for her crime. She never paid it.

A Quaker
Upbringing

Susan Brownell Anthony was born on February 15, 1820, in the rural town of Adams, Massachusetts. Her father, Daniel Anthony, had been raised a Quaker. Quakers are the Religious Society of Friends, which had originated in the mid-1600s in England. Quakers have strict ideals by which they live. They are quiet and somber—no loud voices or singing. They dress mostly in grays—no colorful or frilly garb. Quakers do not believe that priests or places of worship are necessary to have a relationship with God. Instead, Quakers believe that every person has an "inner light" that is able to direct them to divine truth. Quakers were one of the first organized groups to practice complete equality between men and women. Quakers also do not believe in war (armed conflict) or slavery.

Susan's mother, Lucy Read, had been raised a Baptist. Baptists do gather at a church to listen to sermons and pray. Lucy had liked to sing and dance and wear brightly colored clothes. The Anthonys and the Reads, both farming families, were neighbors. Living next door to each other, Daniel and Lucy became fast childhood friends and remained so as they grew up together. In his teenage years, Daniel left Adams to attend school. When he returned, he and Lucy soon discovered that their friendship had turned into love. Daniel loved Lucy's zeal for life and happy nature. Eager to begin a life together, they got married. The young couple, however, did not take the time to obtain official Quaker approval of the marriage, and a scandal resulted.

Daniel's formal apology to the congregation stated that "I am sorry that in order to marry the woman I love best, I had to violate a rule of the religious society I revered the most."[1] The Society accepted his apology, and Daniel was able to regain his status within the community. Lucy felt badly about the Quakers' reaction to the marriage, and she became withdrawn and quiet. And although Lucy took on the ways of the Quakers—no longer singing and dancing or wearing bright clothing—she never became a Quaker herself. Daniel and Lucy loved each other deeply and tried to make the best of the situation. In her biography of Susan B. Anthony, Kathleen Barry notes that "Lucy Anthony learned to be pious and humble as a young bride, and soon she would pass these virtues on to her daughters."[2]

CHILDHOOD DAYS

Following their wedding, Daniel and Lucy lived for a brief time with Lucy's parents. Lucy's mother gave the young couple some land on the Berkshire range on which they decided to build a house. So while living with Lucy's parents, Daniel spent his time building a large farmhouse for him and his new bride. He used lumber from his father in exchange for work Daniel had done for him. When the newlyweds were able to move in, they quickly transformed the farmhouse into a place to call home.

Although Lucy never fully recovered from the scandal that surrounded her marriage and she remained reserved for the rest of her life, Lucy was fiercely devoted to her family. All of the Anthony children knew the love and com mitment their mother felt toward them.

Daniel and Lucy had six children who survived infancy. Susan was the second. There were four girls and two boys. Guelma was born first, in 1818. After Susan was born in 1820, Hannah arrived in 1821, Daniel in 1824, Mary in 1827, and J. Merritt in 1834. Another daughter, Ann Eliza, died as an infant in 1833, and another child did not survive childbirth. The Anthony children, who grew up as devout Quakers, studied God's word daily. Following Quaker tradition, Daniel and Lucy did not allow toys or music in the home, as they were considered distractions from the children's education and upbringing. Daniel and Lucy took an active role in standing up for their beliefs—especially concerning education and equality among all people, regardless of race or sex. Because of these beliefs, Susan and her sisters and brothers grew up with a strong sense of justice. They were each taught self-reliance, self-discipline, and self-worth.

When Susan was four years old, she and her sisters Guelma and Hannah went to live briefly with their paternal grandparents while Lucy gave birth to Daniel. During Susan's time with her grandparents, Grandfather Anthony taught Guelma and Susan to read. The girls spent long hours each day on their studies, reading countless books. When the girls returned home after Daniel's birth, Lucy noticed that Susan's eyes appeared slightly crossed and her vision seemed distorted. After a few weeks' rest from reading, Susan's vision improved, much to her mother's relief.

Susan, however, would continue to have trouble reading, and her left eye would remain slightly crossed for the rest of her life.

In 1822, Daniel took on a new venture. He built and operated a cotton mill across the street from his farm. He hired teenage girls to work in the mill. Half of these girls boarded in the house with Daniel, Lucy, and the children. As a result, the house that Susan and her siblings grew up in was always bustling. Biographers Geoffrey Ward and Ken Burns described Susan's house duties as "an almost ceaseless round of work—sewing, cleaning, hauling water, preparing three meals a day for as many as sixteen people, and washing up again once they had finished eating."[3] Despite all the domestic chores that kept the Anthony children busy indoors, they also enjoyed exploring the land around their farm and mill in the Berkshire Hills. Biographer Barry explained, "In winter, [the Anthony children] played in the fresh deep snows, sometimes running out to catch snowflakes. In summer, they might set across the open rolling hills for an afternoon of picking wildflowers or just walking. Often Susan sat in the grass behind their house and watched the sunset behind the looming Mount Greylock. She was enchanted with nature and could sit in wonder over the workings of a community of insects or nursing a wounded bird back to flight."[4]

Daniel's mill and farm were flourishing. Just four years after Daniel opened his mill, John McLean, a New York judge, approached Daniel with a proposition. McLean had seen how successful Daniel's mill had become in such a short time. He told Daniel that he would supply the capital if Daniel would move to Battenville, New York, and start an industrial community there. Daniel considered the offer and decided it was a good one. So in 1826, the Anthonys packed up and moved to Battenville, about 35 miles (56 kilometers) north of Albany. Susan was six years old at the time. Over the next 10 years, Daniel would transform the small village into a prosperous town. In 1832, Daniel built a 15-room house for his large family. The Anthonys' new house was a huge brick dwelling that also included a store and a schoolroom.

FROM STUDENT TO TEACHER

It was in this schoolroom that Susan and her siblings received much of their education. They had briefly tried public education, but Daniel had taken them out when Susan complained that her teacher (a man) had refused to teach her long division because she was a girl. Daniel himself taught the children for a while, but then he found Mary Perkins, a woman who used teaching methods that were innovative for the time. For example, Perkins included calisthenics, books with pictures, and poetry recitation in her learning day.

In 1837, when Susan was 17 years old, Daniel enrolled her in a Quaker boarding school called Deborah Moulson's Female Seminary, located near Philadelphia. He had sent Guelma there first—she had been able to earn her tuition by working as a teaching assistant. Neither Guelma nor Susan asked why they could not attend a college, as the boys did. They felt fortunate to be able to receive any additional schooling.

Around this time, however, the Panic of 1837 swept the country. The economic depression caused Daniel Anthony to declare bankruptcy, and the family lost their house in Battenville. He could no longer afford the boarding school tuition, and Susan—following her one term at the school—was forced to withdraw. Susan had not been happy at the all-girls school, however; she had been terribly homesick and lonely. She had become depressed and withdrawn, refusing to spend time getting to know the other girls. Moulson was strict and humiliated the young

Lucretia Mott worked to organize the Philadelphia Female Anti-Slavery Society in 1833. Her niece, Lydia Mott, and Susan B. Anthony became friends when they attended Deborah Moulson's Female Seminary near Philadelphia in 1837. Lucretia Mott would sometimes speak to the students at the school.

women by dwelling on their mistakes. Susan did eventually make some friends at the school, including Lydia Mott, the niece of Lucretia Mott. Lucretia was a Quaker abolitionist who sometimes came to the school to speak to the students about the importance of education. Still, most memories of the seminary were unpleasant for Susan, and she willingly left it behind to return to her family.

In 1839, the Anthonys moved again—this time to Hardscrabble (later called Center Falls), New York, where the family rented a tavern. Daniel and Lucy took in boarders to cover the rent of the tavern. Also at this time, their oldest daughter, Guelma, married Aaron McLean, the son of John McLean.

Susan, on the other hand, left home to take a teaching position that would allow her to contribute money to ease the family's financial troubles. Susan had not always dreamed of being a teacher. In an interview with Nellie Bly that appeared in the February 2, 1896, edition of the New York *World*, Susan told her, "As a little girl my highest ideal was to be a Quaker minister. I wanted to be inspired by God to speak in church. That was my highest ambition. My father believed in educating his girls so they could be self-supporting if necessary. In olden times there was only one [career] open to women. That was teaching. So every one of us girls took turns at teaching. I began when I was fifteen and taught until I was thirty."[5] And so, with her family in need, Susan set aside her desire to become a Quaker minister and took an assistant teacher position at Eunice Kenyon's Friends' Seminary, a Quaker boarding school, in New Rochelle, New York.

Here, Susan became fast friends with Eunice, who exposed Susan to different teaching methods (Eunice was lenient and Susan was strict) and disciplinary techniques (Eunice was relaxed and Susan was harsh). Susan enjoyed her time teaching here, though she deeply missed her family. In particular, Susan missed Guelma, with whom she had always been close. Susan felt that they had drifted apart—not only physically, but emotionally as well—since Guelma's marriage to Aaron.

In 1845, Susan's younger sister Hannah became engaged to Eugene Mosher. Once again, Susan felt the same loss that she had when Guelma married. The three eldest Anthony sisters had spent all their young lives as best friends. They had shared their thoughts, hopes, and dreams with one another. Neither Guelma nor Hannah continued the close contact once they married; Susan suddenly felt painfully alone.

CANAJOHARIE ACADEMY

Daniel and Lucy Anthony were gradually recovering from the economic depression of 1837. They purchased a farm in Gates, just west of Rochester, New York. Susan B. Anthony, done with her work at Eunice Kenyon's Friends' Seminary, lived at the farm, helping to run the place.

Anthony was 26 years old when she accepted her next teaching position. The year was 1846; she would earn just over $100 for the entire year's work. Anthony's position was the head of the girls' department at Canajoharie Academy. She stayed with the school for three years. Canajoharie was a beautiful town on the Mohawk River in New York. Anthony first boarded with her Uncle Joshua and then with her cousin Margaret Caldwell. At the start of the school year, Anthony worried that she would feel unqualified. Until now, she had worked only with young students and as an assistant teacher. At Canajoharie, the students were at high school level. Despite her fears, Anthony proved to be a competent, well-respected teacher.

A year into teaching at Canajoharie, Anthony began to accumulate money of her own. Her parents no longer needed financial help; their farm was flourishing, and they had begun to rebuild their financial security. Anthony discovered that she had money to spend on pretty things, like beautiful dresses in the latest styles. She began to turn the heads of young men. One man, Mr. Loaux, visited with Anthony several times; she enjoyed his company. But then he suddenly stopped coming—with no explanation. Other men courted Anthony as well, and although a few proposed, she never accepted a proposal of marriage. She later said, "I never felt I could give up my life of freedom to become a man's housekeeper. When I was young, if a girl married poor she became a housekeeper and a drudge. If she married wealthy, she became a pet and a doll."[6]

Still, Anthony did not make a conscious decision to remain unmarried; it simply happened that way. In 1896, she told an interviewer who had asked her why she refused the proposals of marriage she received: "It was simply that I never met a man whom I thought I loved well enough to live with all my life, and for that matter, I never met one whom I thought loved me well enough to live with me all his life. That marriage proposition has two sides. Probably I'd have been very trying to live with."[7] Although she was not finding someone to marry, Anthony enjoyed spending time with the young men who called on her.

In 1848, Anthony heard about a controversial woman named Elizabeth Cady Stanton, who had teamed up with Lucretia Mott. Back in 1833, Mott had formed the Philadelphia Female Anti-Slavery Society. She had long been an outspoken advocate for reform. In 1840, Mott traveled to London, England, to attend the World Anti-Slavery Conference. Also trying to get into the convention was Stanton. Mott and Stanton were refused permission to attend because they were women. Furious, the two women decided to create their own convention, but it would be several years before it would come to pass.

Together, they organized the Seneca Falls Woman's Rights Convention, which would meet over two days, July 19 and 20 in 1848, "to discuss the social, civil and religious

This group of life-size bronze statues is the signature piece of art at the Women's Rights National Historical Park in Seneca Falls, New York. The statues depict *(from left)* Elizabeth Cady Stanton, Frederick Douglass, Lucretia Mott, and others who attended the 1848 Woman's Rights Convention at Seneca Falls. The convention put forth a Declaration of Sentiments stating 12 rights to be granted to women.

condition and rights of Women."[8] They stated 12 rights that they wished to see granted for women in a Declaration of Sentiments. These rights included ones that men already enjoyed—owning property, keeping wages you earn, speaking in public, obtaining custody of children in the event of divorce, and voting. Reaction to the convention by the press was mostly critical. In their biography on Stanton and Anthony, Ward and Burns quote the *Philadelphia Public Ledger and Daily Transcript* as saying, "A woman is nobody. A wife is everything. … A pretty girl is equal to ten thousand men, and a mother is, next to God, all powerful. ... The ladies of Philadelphia, therefore, under the influence of the most serious, sober second thoughts, are resolved to maintain their rights as Wives, Belles, Virgins and Mothers, and not as Women."[9]

Stanton was not put off by the poor publicity. She saw it as another tool in spreading the word for her cause. She hoped that the articles written about the convention—negative or positive—would get more women thinking about their rights. Following the convention, Stanton organized follow-up meetings in various cities. One of those cities was Rochester, New York. Anthony's youngest sister, Mary, attended the meetings along with Daniel and Lucy Anthony. Mary later shared her findings with Susan, who was teaching at Canajoharie at the time.

PUBLIC SPEAKING

During her time at Canajoharie, Anthony joined the Daughters of Temperance, a group of women who drew attention to the effects of drunkenness on families and campaigned for stronger liquor laws. The Anthony family had long believed that drinking liquor was sinful, and they were strong advocates of temperance, which is abstinence from alcoholic drink. Anthony made her first public speech in 1849 at a Daughters of Temperance supper. She spoke about the corrupt influence of alcohol. She told her audience that women needed to bring reform and new moral standards to society. Anthony felt excited and alive when she spoke. She had never before felt like this—not when she worked on her family's farm, not when she taught at school, and not when she was on a date with a young man. When Anthony was speaking in front of people about ideas that she believed in and felt a passion for, she experienced a newfound energy and fulfillment.

Three weeks following this stimulating speech, Anthony resigned from her position at Canajoharie. She was ready to make a change in the world—she would begin by leaving teaching behind. Perhaps she would continue to make speeches as she had at the Daughters of Temperance supper. She was not exactly sure what she wanted, but she knew that what she wanted did not include teaching day after day. She would go home to rest a bit and then decide what direction to take with her life.

But when her cousin, Margaret Caldwell, with whom Anthony had been living, became ill, Anthony's plans changed. Since Caldwell was pregnant with her fifth child, Anthony did not want to leave her alone. She decided to keep on at the school a bit longer so that she could nurse Caldwell. Anthony did not get along with Margaret's husband, Joseph Caldwell. Anthony thought that he was selfish and unsupportive, and did not deserve Margaret. After Margaret gave birth to a baby girl, Margaret remained unwell and bedridden for seven weeks. Anthony stayed on with her during this time, rather than return home to her

IN HER OWN WORDS

The passion and drive that Susan B. Anthony first experienced speaking before the Daughters of Temperance supper would continue for the rest of her life. In an 1895 interview, as cited in Lynn Sherr's *Failure Is Impossible*, Anthony said:

How do I keep so energetic? By always being busy, by never having time to think of myself, and never indulging in any form of self-absorption.

parents. Sadly, Margaret did not make it; she passed away. Anthony took the loss hard. She felt lonely, depressed, and confused. No longer clear about the direction she wanted to take in her life, Anthony returned home to her parents' farm in Gates.

The Power
of Reform

Susan B. Anthony worked on her family's farm, finding enjoyment in gardening and other chores. But she found herself attending temperance and anti-slavery meetings so often that her gardens started to look neglected. Her sister Mary told Anthony that she hoped, "When you get a husband and children, you will treat them better than you did your raspberry plants, and not leave them to their fate at the beginning of winter."[1] Anthony did not have her mind on a husband or children, however. Biographers Geoffrey Ward and Ken Burns said, "[Anthony] joined the local Daughters of Temperance soon after moving to Rochester and before long was organizing suppers and fairs, then traveling to neighboring towns to show other women how to do the same. From the first, she exhibited organizational skills and a willingness to work that soon earned her the nickname 'Napoleon.'"[2] In setting up lectures and speaking out on issues that were important to her, Anthony had found a calling, one she could see herself doing for the rest of her life—whereas tending the farm and gardens, while enjoyable, did nothing for Anthony's intellectual needs.

FINDING A PURPOSE THROUGH REFORM

Anthony realized that she needed to make some important decisions regarding her life. She wanted to make a serious commitment; she chose social-reform work. In a letter Anthony wrote in 1848, she said, "I am tired of theory. I want to hear how we must act to have a happier and more glorious world. ... Reform, reform needs to be the watch word. And somebody must preach it, who does not depend on the popular nod for his dinner."[3] One small step for women's rights that year was the Married Woman's Property Act, which allowed women to inherit money in their own right. Unfortunately, this act did not give women the right to keep the money they earned themselves. So a woman who held a job was still expected to hand her wages over to her husband at the end of the day. This became one of many issues Anthony would later tackle in her lifelong reform work.

At this time, the entire country was deep into the debate over slavery. Daniel and Lucy Anthony had spent much of their lives supporting the cause of abolitionism, working to end slavery, and the entire family became active in the anti-slavery movement. They helped runaway slaves make their way along the Underground Railroad. Nearly every Sunday, interested Quakers would travel from miles away to talk about the movement at the Anthony home. Well-known abolitionists Frederick Douglass and William Lloyd Garrison were at these meetings on occasion. Susan's

Anti-slavery Quakers would often meet at the Anthony family home in Rochester, New York, to discuss events in the movement. There, during one such gathering, Susan B. Anthony met Frederick Douglass *(above)*, the famous abolitionist.

brothers, Daniel and Merritt, would travel to Kansas in 1856 to support anti-slavery activities; there, the brothers supported John Brown, an abolitionist who was fighting pro-slavery forces.

Anthony listened intently at these anti-slavery events and often felt moved by the speakers, especially William Lloyd Garrison and George Thompson, two of the most radical abolitionists. Anthony felt that she could identify with their arguments. Around this time, Quaker aboli-

FREDERICK DOUGLASS

Frederick Douglass (born Frederick Augustus Washington Bailey) was the son of a slave woman and an unknown white man. Douglass was born in Maryland in February 1818. His mother died when he was seven years old. After his mother's death, Douglass was sent to Baltimore to live with a man named Hugh Auld, a ship carpenter. Auld's wife taught Douglass how to read. But when Douglass was 15, he was sent to live with Edward Covey, a farmer. There, Douglass received daily whippings and little food.

After a failed attempt at escape, Douglass was able to get to Massachusetts in 1838. He started to attend abolitionists' meetings and gave a speech at the Massachusetts Anti-Slavery Society's annual convention in Nantucket. Douglass spent his life trying to better the lives of African Americans.

Susan B. Anthony first met Douglass at her family's home in Rochester when she was in her 20s. Douglass would join the group of anti-slavery Quakers who met to discuss what was happening in the country. Anthony also read his writings about slavery in his publication called *North Star*. Douglass was such an important friend to the family that he would later deliver the eulogy at the funeral of Anthony's father. Anthony herself would one day read a eulogy at Douglass's funeral in 1895.

tionists Stephen and Abby Foster asked Anthony to join the anti-slavery movement. Anthony, however, was not yet ready to tackle such a complicated political issue. She felt she wanted to learn more about what made slavery such an entrenched economic institution before she could fully join in the discussions. Anthony did not like to be on the outskirts of a topic; she wanted to be in the midst of it—and she wanted to be fully educated and ready before putting herself in that position.

A FRIENDSHIP IS BORN

In 1849, Anthony met Amelia Bloomer, an editor for *The Lily*, the first woman-owned newspaper in the United States. Anthony soon started to write articles on temperance for the newspaper. Her involvement with the paper allowed her a chance to meet other female participants in the abolitionist and women's movements. One woman whom Anthony started to hear a lot more about—both from friends and from articles she read in the newspaper— was Elizabeth Cady Stanton. Anthony admired Stanton's work and hoped one day to meet her.

In May 1851, Anthony traveled to Syracuse, New York, to attend an anti-slavery convention. There, she listened to Garrison and Thompson. After Syracuse, Anthony traveled to nearby Seneca Falls, where Bloomer lived. Bloomer had invited Anthony to stay with her so that Anthony could hear Garrison and Thompson again when their lecture tour arrived there. Anthony was excited about the visit, in part because she knew that Bloomer and Stanton were friends. Anthony still hoped to meet the outspoken woman.

Anthony finally got her chance. After the lecture, Bloomer and Anthony stood outside amid other guests. Bloomer spotted Stanton, and introductions were made. At the time, however, Stanton had other social arrangements on her mind—Garrison and Thompson were to be house-guests at her home that evening. So the long-awaited meeting was brief. Nonetheless, it was the beginning of what would become a lifelong friendship. Sara Evans, in her book *Born for Liberty: A History of Women in America*, notes that "the partnership between Stanton and Anthony brought together a brilliant organizer, Anthony, with a charismatic speaker and writer, Stanton. It allowed Stanton to continue her activism in the midst of a complex domestic life."[4]

Soon after, Stanton invited Anthony to stay with her during a meeting she planned to have with activist Lucy Stone and journalist Horace Greeley to discuss coeducational college. Anthony gladly accepted the invitation and arrived at Stanton's home eager to finally have a chance to better understand the person she admired.

Now that they were able to spend more time together and get to know each other, Stanton and Anthony learned that they were a good match of wits and intellect. Stanton was a busy mother of four boys and would eventually have three more children—two girls and another boy. Stanton's husband, Henry, was frequently away doing political work, leaving Elizabeth and Susan to form a close bond.

Stanton's motherhood would come to put some strain on their relationship, because Anthony believed that women fighting for suffrage should devote their entire lives to the cause, and she saw marriage and children as a distraction. Nonetheless, Stanton and Anthony seemed destined to change the world together. Late in Stanton's life, she would remember their partnership: "In writing we did better work together than either could alone. While she is slow and analytical in composition, I am rapid and synthetic. I am the better writer, she the better critic. She supplied the facts and statistics, I the philosophy and rhetoric, and together we have made arguments that have stood unshaken by the storms of thirty long years; arguments that no man has answered."[5]

In January 1852, Anthony attended a Sons of Temperance meeting in Rochester. She had been asked to be a delegate at this statewide convention. Before the meeting, Anthony had worked hard to collect signatures petitioning to ban the sale and production of liquor. At the meeting, Anthony rose to speak about her thoughts and ideas on temperance. The chairperson—a man—instructed Anthony to join the other women and keep quiet while the men conducted their meeting. This attitude went against Anthony's Quaker upbringing. She tried to remain quiet, but eventually she felt a need to speak. When she tried, she was immediately told to "listen and learn."[6] Anthony was not going to stand for this discrimination, and she left the meeting at once.

Unhappy with how she had been treated at the meeting, Anthony decided to take matters into her own hands. She organized the Women's State Temperance Society—one that would be organized and run by women. And Anthony asked her new friend, Stanton, to act as the society's first president.

The women had much to tackle—not only temperance. In the early and mid-1800s, women had few rights. In fact, a married woman had no legal rights. She could not own property, she could not keep the money she earned, she could not be named guardian of her children. If she tried to leave her husband, she could be brought back and beaten. If a husband decided to leave his wife, he could do so—and take the children with him. No woman could go to college. Women who did work earned significantly less than their male coworkers did. Women could not become doctors, lawyers, or senators. And no woman could vote. When one minister tried to tell Anthony that she should be married with a large family, she responded, "I thought it was much better for me to devote my life to amending the State law which denied mothers the right of guardianship of their own children, than for me to be the mother of a half-dozen children who were not legally my own."[7]

THE BLOOMER

The year 1852 brought with it a bold new look for women's rights activists. Elizabeth Smith Miller had designed an avant-garde outfit that consisted of a short skirt, full trousers, and a cloak that reached to the knee. Miller was the daughter of Gerrit Smith (a famous abolitionist) and a cousin of Elizabeth Cady Stanton. Miller described how she came to create the forward-thinking outfit in this way: "In the spring of 1851, while spending many hours at work in the garden, I became so thoroughly disgusted with the long skirt, that the dissatisfaction—the growth of years—suddenly ripened into the decision that this shackle should no longer be endured. The resolution was at once put into practice. Turkish trousers to the ankle with a skirt reaching some four inches below the knee, were substituted for the heavy, untidy, and exasperating old garment."[8]

When Miller showed the new outfit to Stanton, she was thrilled. Miller noted that Stanton "at once joined me in wearing the new costume."[9] Stanton and Miller showed the outfit to Amelia Bloomer, Stanton's friend and neighbor. Bloomer described the outfit in her newspaper, *The Lily*, and continued to promote it on a regular basis. Her constant advertising of this daring new look caused it to become known as "the Bloomer."

Anthony was slow to wear the new Bloomer, though she did—about six months after Stanton started to wear it. Anthony even cut off her long hair into a short bob. In a letter to Lucy Stone, Anthony wrote, "The dress question I pass over, fully agreeing with you that woman can never

This Currier and Ives lithograph shows the Bloomer costume, which some women began to wear in the 1850s. The outfit was considered daring, and many thought it was inappropriate. Susan B. Anthony wore the Bloomer for about a year but gave it up because she thought the attention it received distracted from the causes she was advocating.

compete successfully with men in the various industrial avocations, in long skirts. No one knows their bondage save the few of us who have known the freedom of short skirts."[10] Years later, in 1895, Anthony said in a speech, "If you are going to act wisely, you want a costume to suit the occasion. If a woman goes into a factory with spindles flying, she does not want lace down on her wrists nor flounces on her dress. Yet some men talk as if the world were coming to an end because of this very natural evolution."[11]

In the end, Anthony felt that the Bloomer took the focus away from the cause, as people became too engrossed in forming their opinion on whether the outfit was appropriate. Every time Anthony walked down the street, people jeered and stared at her. Men made rude comments. Anthony was never frightened by the attention her appearance drew, but it caused her to grow emotionally drained and on edge. Anthony did not care for any distraction from her work and so after just over a year of wearing the Bloomer, she went back to plain, long dresses, usually gray or black. Sharing her mother's love of bright colors, however, Anthony insisted on one spot of color—a red shawl, which she often wore when she lectured.

THE WOMEN'S STATE TEMPERANCE SOCIETY

The Women's State Temperance Society quickly grew to 500 members. Its first meeting was held on April 20, 1852, in Corinthian Hall in Rochester, New York. Stanton, acting as president, spoke to the delegates. She wore the new Bloomer, which Amelia Bloomer would describe in the June 1852 issue of *The Lily* as a "rich black satin dress, a plain waist after the prevailing style of ladies' dresses, full skirt falling six or eight inches below the knee, plain wide trousers of the same material, and black 'congress' gaiters. On her neck, a fine linen cambrick collar, fastened with a gold pin, and cuffs of same material about her wrist."[12]

Stanton believed that it was important to change the laws regarding divorce. At the time, the only way a person could divorce a spouse was on the grounds of adultery. Stanton wanted a woman to be allowed to file for divorce if her husband was abusing alcohol. She told the delegates, "Let no woman remain in the relation of wife with a confirmed drunkard. ... Let no drunkard be the father of her children."[13]

Reaction to Stanton's statements was mixed, but those who opposed her beliefs were angry. Stanton was unable to respond after the convention, however, because she was pregnant with her fifth child. She did not like to be in the public eye during her pregnancies, so she stayed out of the spotlight in her home in Seneca Falls. Anthony stepped up to face the reaction and carry on with the duties of the Women's State Temperance Society. She had become its general agent and had encouraged the delegates to not allow men to vote or hold positions in the society. Anthony organized meetings (men were allowed to attend), raised funds, and gave lectures.

Anthony was used to dealing with angry people. She stood by her beliefs and remained calm and collected. She did become discouraged, however, when, in 1852, she was traveling to speak on temperance and found that many clergymen would not allow her to lecture in their churches. Anthony was losing the chance to reach hundreds of people. In a letter Anthony wrote that year, she said, "The power of the clergy over the minds of the people, particularly the women, is truly alarming. I am every day, more and more made to feel the importance of woman's being educated to 'lean not upon man but upon her own understanding.' The question now, with the masses of the women, is not whether they may be instrumental in doing good to society by engaging in the temperance we propose to them, but will the minister approve the plan of action."[14] Despite these obstacles, Anthony never slowed her pace or let discouragement get the best of her. She was forever looking ahead to the next battle.

WE STAND HERE TO BE HEARD

In September 1852, Anthony attended her first Woman's Rights Convention. She listened to speeches by Antoinette Brown, Lucy Stone, and Ernestine Rose—all well known to the women's rights movement. Although Anthony was not yet known for her women's rights activities, she was recognized for her work in temperance. Not timid, Anthony stood up at the convention and spoke in a loud, clear voice about the importance of colleges admitting women, about women having the right to stop attending a church that did not treat them equally, and about the importance of women being heard. "We do not stand up here to be seen," she said, "but to be heard."[15]

In June 1853, Anthony and Stanton were ready to hold the second annual convention of the Women's State Temperance Society, once again in Rochester. Membership had risen from the original 500 to a force of 2,000 delegates. Unfortunately for Anthony and Stanton, the majority of members wanted to redirect the society's focus back to temperance and stop talk about women's rights and changing divorce laws. Stanton addressed the concerns:

> It has been objected that we do not confine ourselves to the subject of temperance, but talk too much about woman's rights, divorce and the church. … We have been obliged to preach woman's rights because many, instead of listening have questioned the right of woman to speak on any subject. … Let it be clearly understood that we are a Woman's Rights Society; that we believe it is a woman's duty to speak

whenever she feels the impression to do so; that it is her right to be present in all the councils of Church and State.[16]

Despite Stanton's plea to continue fighting for women's rights, the members of the Women's State Temperance Society held their ground. Delegates voted Stanton out as president. Anthony was upset by their decision. Like Stanton, she believed that they needed to look at more than just temperance. She decided to stand by her friend. Anthony resigned from her position in the society to show her displeasure with the treatment of Stanton. Anthony was sorry to leave the Temperance Society, which she had built from scratch. But she believed in Stanton's point about needing to focus on a larger picture—alcohol was only a small part of the change these women felt needed to be made.

At the New York State Teachers Convention in 1853, Anthony attended three days' worth of sessions. Anthony was interested in learning what would be done to upgrade schools. She hoped to see improvements in teaching and sanitary issues. She asked that female teachers earn better pay and sought for women to have a voice at the convention and to assume committee positions. She wanted to see women allowed to study for occupations that were not available, like medicine and law.

During the meeting, the male delegates were speaking about the lack of respect that the profession of teaching received. When the men refused to let Anthony speak until they had completed the official voting, she stood up to speak anyway: "It seems to me, gentlemen, that none of you quite comprehend the cause of the disrespect of which you complain. Do you not see that as long as society says a woman is incompetent to be a lawyer, minister, or doctor, but has ample ability to be a teacher, that every man of you who chooses this profession tacitly acknowledges that he has no more brains than a woman?"[17]

In 1854, Anthony would have her chance to address her unhappiness with the Married Woman's Property Act, which had passed in 1848. Although this act allowed women to inherit money, it did not allow women to keep their wages. Anthony wanted to see that provision changed. She wrote in her journal, "Woman must have a purse of her own, and how can this be so long as the law denies to the wife all right to both the individual and the joint earnings?"[18] Once again, Anthony asked Stanton to prepare a speech that would state what women wanted: to keep their wages and gain the right to vote. Anthony organized an effort to obtain signatures on petitions asking for these rights. The women organized the State Woman's Rights Convention in Albany, New York, to be held on February 14 and 15, 1854. Stanton delivered the first speech by a woman in the New York legislature. She, Anthony, and suffragist Ernestine Rose had gathered 10,000 signatures, which they presented to the legislature.

Anthony printed 50,000 copies of Stanton's speech and distributed them throughout the state of New York. She ensured, too, that a copy of the speech was available to each state legislator. Anthony and Rose also made speeches to legislative committees. When the legislators failed to take action, Anthony stepped up. She and Rose traveled to Washington, D.C.; Baltimore, Maryland; and Alexandria, Virginia. During this trip, Anthony had her first look at what slavery was really like in the South. It sickened and saddened her. It also left her wanting to speak out against slavery and to encourage people to fight for the equality of all people. She returned from her trip on October 1 and immediately started to make plans for another tour, this time one that would keep her in New York. This trip would be dedicated to campaigning for married women's property rights.

So on Christmas Day, December 25, 1854, Anthony started off on a five-month road trip to make speeches all over New York. Her first lecture was on December 26, and then she scheduled a lecture every other day from there on out. To pay for her trains, carriages, and inns, she charged 25 cents to people to listen to her speak. Still, Anthony was often short of money. She frequently used her own money to pay for her food and travel expenses.

People came in droves to hear Anthony lecture during these early months in 1855. Some people came because they had never before heard a woman speak in public. Others came because they believed in what Anthony was preaching. One woman who heard Anthony speak later wrote in her diary, "[Susan B. Anthony] had a large audience and she talked plainly about [women's] rights and how we ought to stand up for them and said the world would never go right until the women had just as much right to vote and rule as men. She asked us all to come up and sign our names who would promise to do all in our power to bring about that glad day. ... A whole lot of us went up and signed the paper."[19]

Anthony's dedication to her beliefs and her commanding speaking abilities captivated audiences and reform leaders alike. In 1856, Anthony was asked to become a New York state agent for the American Anti-Slavery Society. Reformer Samuel May had told her, "The Anti-Slavery Society wants you in the field. I really think the efficiency and success of our operation in New York this winter will depend more on your personal attendance and direction than upon that of any other of our workers. We need your earnestness, your practical talent, your energy and perseverance to make these conventions successful.

This portrait of Susan B. Anthony was taken around 1850. She had just started to devote her life to social-reform work. By the mid-1850s, Anthony was attracting crowds of people to hear her speak. Anthony's speaking abilities and her dedication to her beliefs captivated audiences, whether she was discussing women's rights, temperance, or abolition.

The public mind will be sore this winter, disappointment awaits vast numbers, dismay will overtake many. We want your cheerfulness, your spirit—in short, yourself."[20] Anthony accepted the request under the condition that she could continue her women's rights activities. The society agreed. Anthony would earn $10 a week working for the Anti-Slavery Society. She arranged meetings, made speeches, put up posters, and distributed leaflets. Susan B. Anthony was doing what she was best at: standing up for her beliefs and not backing down.

Breaking Down
Fences

Susan B. Anthony was leading a busy life since joining the women's rights movement in 1852. By the mid-1850s, Anthony had dedicated her life to women's rights and working to bring an end to slavery. Anthony believed that granting women the right to vote would solve many problems—like equal pay and coeducation. When prompted with a comment that women do not want to vote during a speech Anthony made in 1871, she responded: "I don't believe it. ... Then why do men put the words 'white males' into their Constitutions? ... Men don't fence a corn field because the pigs don't want the corn, but because they, themselves, do. They fence the field to keep the pigs out."[1] Anthony hoped to break these fences down.

But while Anthony was dedicating her life to breaking down fences, not everyone held her level of commitment. Each time one of the women's rights leaders got married or had a baby, Anthony felt that they were betraying the cause. Anthony thought that women committed to the cause should not waste their time and energies with such distractions as marriage and children. Not that Anthony felt *all* women should abandon marriage and children—simply the front leaders. In a speech she gave in 1897, Anthony told the women of the audience, "It is not necessary for you to be a public speaker or to go on the platform. Every woman in her own home can be a teacher of this great principle of equality. She can instruct her husband and her children in the ways of justice toward all."[2]

Yet when it came to good friends, like Elizabeth Cady Stanton, Anthony felt deserted when they chose to marry or have a child. Anthony was shocked when her friend Lucy Stone dropped out of the women's movement to marry abolitionist Henry Blackwell. Anthony had never considered that Stone would let something like marriage end her commitment to the women's cause. And Stanton continued to have to abandon conventions and meetings because of the six children she had had by 1856. In a letter she wrote to Stanton, Anthony said, "Those of you who have the *talent* to do honor to poor—oh! how poor—womanhood, have all given yourselves over to *baby* making and left poor brainless *me* to do battle alone—it is a shame, such a body as *I might* be *spared* to *rock cradles*, but it is a *crime* for *you* & Lucy [Stone] & Nette [Browne]."[3]

WORKING CONVENTIONS

Anthony campaigned for a wide array of issues, including temperance, the abolition of slavery, the rights of women to their own property and earnings, women's labor organiza-

Elizabeth Cady Stanton posed for a portrait in 1856 with her infant daughter Harriot. Stanton, who stayed out of the public eye when she was pregnant, had six children by 1856. Susan B. Anthony sometimes felt abandoned when her fellow women's rights activists chose to marry or have children.

tions, and women's voting rights. Before she took on a new issue, she always made sure that she felt well-schooled on the topic. She did not like to take on a cause unless she felt she deeply understood its intricacies and nuances. Once she mastered an issue and knew where she stood on the topic, she shared her views with the public, hoping to educate and bring about reform.

Anthony was a good strategizer. When she took on a new campaign, she thought about whom she needed to reach and the best way to accomplish that. She rarely rested but kept up vigorous campaign schedules that left little time for anything but travel and speaking. Biographer Kathleen Barry wrote, "[Anthony] cared little about her own comforts nor was she concerned with gaining personal rewards for her work. Success was for the cause—for womankind. She put her own needs and satisfactions aside, and thus she was able to plan strategies and mount campaigns that were finely tuned to the issues and the conditions of women's lives from which the issues were drawn."[4] As she dedicated more and more of her time to campaigning on various issues, Anthony became an influential and esteemed speaker. She remained calm and composed when

DID YOU KNOW?

As Susan B. Anthony made her way across the country to give speeches about women's rights, she often used her own money to pay her expenses. Always strategizing, Anthony usually began her campaign travels in the winter months, enduring harsh temperatures and uncomfortable travel conditions. The reason was that, during the winter, Anthony figured she would receive better attention from farmers, who were not busy in the fields. As a result of Anthony's determination to endure the ruthless weather, she developed problems with her back. Her pain did not stop her, however, from pressing on for the cause.

she was on the platform. She kept her language simple and concise. As a result, she captivated her audiences, winning their attention and respect.

Anthony did not use only lecturing as a tool to get her point across, however. She wrote countless letters to friends, family, politicians, and reporters. To her brother Daniel, Anthony wrote, "You blunder on this question of woman's rights just where thousands of others do. You believe woman unlike man in her nature; that conditions of life which any man of spirit would sooner die than accept are not only endurable to woman but are needful to her fullest enjoyment."[5] Whether through a note to a family member or a letter to an editor of a newspaper, Anthony never missed an opportunity to express her point of view in hopes of bringing about change for the better.

Through her Quaker upbringing, Anthony had been taught that both sexes deserved the same education. To her, there was no other way. In a speech she made in 1856, she tried to reach her audience by pointing out the obvious: "Both sexes eat, sleep, hate, love and desire alike. Everything which relates to the operations of the mind is common to both sexes. ... If they are allowed to attend picnics together, and balls, and dancing schools, and the opera, it certainly will not injure them to use chalk at the same blackboard."[6] The following year, she would bring this same idea to the New York State Teachers' Convention in Binghamton.

There, in 1857, Anthony called for mixed-race education. She told a shocked audience that she thought it was wrong to separate black children from whites. Even more shocking to the audience was that she proposed that women should have the same college opportunities as men. She was met with strong opposition from Charles Davies, a professor of mathematics at West Point, who said that women and men learning together at a college was "a vast social evil ... a monster of social deformity."[7]

Anthony found herself spending more time working with the American Anti-Slavery Society in 1857. Slave masters had obtained more power that year with the Dred Scott decision from the Supreme Court. That ruling decreed that black people were not citizens of the United States; indeed, they had no rights at all. Anthony set up lectures for abolitionists, wrote articles, and spoke up herself. She told her audiences, "Our mission is to deepen sympathy and convert it into right action, to show that men and women of the North are slave-holders, those of the South slave-owners. The guilt rests on the North equally with the South, therefore our work is to rouse the sleeping conscience of the North."[8]

In 1859, Anthony spoke at the state teachers' convention in Troy, New York, and at the teachers' convention in Massachusetts. At both meetings, she argued for coeducation and stressed that there were no differences between the minds of men and women. Anthony called for equal education opportunities for all regardless of race, and for all schools, colleges, and universities to open their doors to women and former slaves. She also campaigned for the right of children of former slaves to attend public schools.

In every speech, Anthony tried to make known her view that women need to be seen and respected as individuals. Over and over again, Anthony spoke out against the view that women were the weaker and frailer sex. Anthony wanted people to recognize that women were capable of being just as smart, strong, and powerful as men. In one speech she made in 1859, she said:

> The true woman will not be exponent of another, or allow another to be such for her. She will be her own individual self, do her own individual work, stand and fall by her own individual wisdom and strength.
> … The old idea that man was made for himself, and

woman for him, that he is the oak, she the vine, he the head, she the heart, he the great conservator of wisdom principle, she of love, will be reverently laid aside with other long since exploded philosophies of the ignorant past. She will proclaim the 'glad tidings of good news' to all women, that women equally with man was made for her own individual happiness.[9]

MARRIED WOMEN'S RIGHTS

In March 1860, Anthony and Stanton would finally come to see closure in the expanded Married Woman's Property Act, for which the women had been fighting for years. The New York legislature planned to vote on whether to pass this expanded act. When Anthony heard this news, she quickly sent Stanton a note saying, "You must move heaven and earth now to secure this bill, and you can if you will only try."[10] Stanton agreed, but she asked Anthony to come to Seneca Falls to give her inspiration while Stanton prepared a speech to give before the legislature's Judicial Committee. Anthony agreed.

Just two weeks later, Stanton, standing tall and proud, delivered a speech to the Judiciary Committee. The women's hard work paid off. The expanded act passed the day after Stanton's speech. Under the new law, women could own property, they could keep their wages, they could partake in business transactions, they could sue and be sued, and they could share custody of their children. After New York adopted this law, other states began to follow. The passing of this expanded act was a true triumph for the women's movement.

Then in May 1860, Stanton would deliver a speech at the tenth annual National Woman's Rights Convention in New York City. There, Stanton would be less well-received. Stanton stated that the laws surrounding marriage were unfair to women and she asked that marriage be a legal contract that either the husband or the wife could end, if so desired. Stanton's words stunned many listeners. The Reverend Antoinette Brown Blackwell was the first to respond to Stanton's speech. She said, "All divorce is naturally and morally impossible."[11] Wendell Phillips tried to have Stanton's words stricken from the official record of the convention. William Lloyd Garrison—although he

ELIZABETH CADY STANTON

Elizabeth Cady Stanton was born in Johnstown, New York, in 1815. She was the eighth of nine children. Five children were girls, and four were boys. Three of those boys died as infants. Elizabeth's surviving brother, Eleazar, became ill and died when he was 20 years old. Elizabeth's father, Daniel Cady, was crushed by his son's death. Elizabeth later wrote about it, "I still recall ... going into the large, darkened parlor to see my brother and finding the casket ... and my father seated by his side, pale and immovable. As he took no notice of me, after standing a long while, I climbed upon his knee, when he mechanically put his arm about me. ... At length, he heaved a deep sigh and said: 'Oh, my daughter, I wish you were a boy!' Throwing my arms about his neck, I replied: 'I will try to be all my brother was.'"*

Stanton would spend much of her life trying to win the approval of her father. She studied at Troy Female Seminary because Union College would not admit female students. After school, Elizabeth met Henry Brewster Stanton, whom she fell in love with and married. She spent her life working toward women's marriage rights, property rights, and voting rights. She was a brilliant writer and was thought to be radical for her time.

did not think Stanton's words needed to be stricken from the record—agreed with Phillips's sentiments. Both men were against Stanton's proposition. Stanton and Anthony were stunned. Anthony had been certain that Garrison and Phillips would agree with their stance.

Anthony had known Stanton for nearly a decade, and the two were as close as sisters. Anthony did not care to see people speak poorly of her friend or her friend's

The friendship between Elizabeth Cady Stanton and Susan B. Anthony was one of greatness. In 1890, Anthony addressed her guests at her seventieth birthday party with these words about her good friend, Stanton, "Mr. Stanton [Elizabeth's husband] was never jealous of any one but [myself], and I think my going to that home many times robbed the children of their rights. But I used to take their little wagon and draw them round the garden while Mrs. Stanton wrote speeches, resolutions, petitions, etc., and I never expect to know any joy in this world equal to that of going up and down, getting good editorials written, engaging halls and advertising Mrs. Stanton's speeches. After that is through with, I don't expect any more joy. If I have ever had any inspiration, she has given it to me. I want you to understand that I never could have done the work I have if I had not had that woman at my right hand."**

*Geoffrey C. Ward and Ken Burns, *Not for Ourselves Alone: The Story of Elizabeth Cady Stanton and Susan B. Anthony.* New York: Alfred A. Knopf, 1999, p. 14.
**Lynn Sherr, *Failure Is Impossible: Susan B. Anthony in Her Own Words.* New York: Random House, 1995, p. 174.

values. Anthony stood by Stanton and defended her beliefs. Anthony told the convention delegates, "Marriage has ever and always will be a one-sided matter, resting most unequally upon the sexes. By it, man gains all—woman loses all; tyrant law and lust remain supreme with him— meek submission, and cheerful, ready obedience, alone befit her. Woman has never been consulted. ... By law, public sentiment and religion, from the time of Moses down to the present day, woman has never been thought of other than as a piece of property, to be disposed of at the will and pleasure of man."[12] Anthony's powerful words did not change the minds of Garrison and Phillips. Anthony wondered if this was the end of their friendship. She could see that her and Stanton's thoughts on divorce had thoroughly riled the men. Anthony hoped the friendships could one day be restored, but for now, she would have to wait and see.

A COUNTRY DIVIDED

As the year 1860 drew to an end, the United States was drawing closer and closer to war. Tensions were high as the country debated the slavery issue. Women's issues—including divorce rights—were seen as secondary during this time of national unrest. It was time to pull together as a nation and put an end to slavery, once and for all. At the start of 1861, Anthony conducted an anti-slavery campaign in New York that began in Buffalo and ended in Albany. The motto of the campaign was, "No Compromise with Slaveholders. Immediate and Unconditional Emancipation."[13] Anthony lined up an impressive list of speakers for the campaign, including Lucretia Mott, Martha Wright, Gerrit Smith, Frederick Douglass, Stephen Foster, and Elizabeth Cady Stanton.

This campaign would prove to be a trying time for Anthony and the others, one that Anthony would later remember as "The Winter of the Mobs." Angry mobs

ANTI-SLAVERY MEETING ON THE COMMON.

This illustration from an 1851 issue of *Gleason's Pictorial Drawing Room Companion* shows Wendell Phillips delivering an anti-slavery speech on the Common in Boston. Besides her women's rights work, Susan B. Anthony was quite active in the anti-slavery movement in the 1850s. As the decade was ending, the fight against slavery was coming to a head.

would try to stop Anthony from speaking out against slavery. They would put out all the gas lamps so that she was left to speak in the dark, call her vile names, or turn off the heat in her lecture hall. One especially hateful evening happened in Syracuse, New York. Anthony and the Reverend Samuel May were speaking together on this particular night. "Rotten eggs were thrown, benches broken, and knives and pistols gleamed in every direction."[14] Later that night, the angry mobs carried effigies—doll-like figures made to look like a particular person—of Anthony and May through the town. The mobs stopped at the center of town and set the effigies on fire. Cheering, the mobs dragged the burning "bodies" through the streets. Anthony stayed strong. She never considered stopping her lectures. The fight must go on.

The American Civil War and Its Aftermath

The American Civil War began in 1861 when guns fired on Fort Sumter in South Carolina. Susan B. Anthony strongly supported the Union during the war. She worried about President Abraham Lincoln's ability to be strong, and she did not fully trust him. He had just been elected president by a narrow vote and stated in his inaugural address that he had no plans to interfere with slavery. Lincoln hoped that a quick military involvement would return order to the nation. Little did he know then that the Civil War would continue for the next four years.

THE WAR BEGINS

Once the war started, the Anti-Slavery Society, headed by William Lloyd Garrison, stopped its public campaigning and lecturing. Anthony thought this was a bad decision. She told a friend, "Our position, to me, seems most humiliating ... simply that of the political world, one of expediency not principle."[1] Not only did Anthony have to stop her abolitionist lecturing, but she also had to put a stop to the National Woman's Rights Convention planned for that May. With the nation's attention focused on the war, there was no one left to speak at or attend the convention. Anthony was devastated.

DID YOU KNOW?

Susan B. Anthony was a woman of action. She believed in getting things done by doing them. She believed in changing wrongs to rights. Sometimes this meant standing in lecture halls and talking to people about social reform. Sometimes it meant writing articles and letters to politicians to ask for laws to protect the rights of a particular group of people. Other times, it meant removing people from bad situations and helping them to safety. For example, over the years, Anthony helped many women get away from abusive husbands. She also helped slaves escape by way of the Underground Railroad. One of the few places we learn about Anthony's involvement with the Underground Railroad is through her diary. In 1861, Anthony wrote, "The last load of hay is in the barn; all in capital order. Fitted out a fugitive slave for Canada with the help of Harriet Tubman."* Although her diary entry is brief and casual, her entry conveys Anthony's bravery and dedication to abolition. Anthony believed in people's freedom and equality.

*Lynn Sherr, *Failure Is Impossible: Susan B. Anthony in Her Own Words*. New York: Random House, 1995, p. 33.

Anthony briefly felt relief when Garrison and the Anti-Slavery Society came to see that it was, in fact, a good idea to stay in the public eye and continue to campaign for the immediate emancipation of slaves, without compromise. Anthony was happy to go back to organizing and lecturing at those meetings.

But Anthony was reminded about the ground being lost to women's rights as a result of the war when, in 1862, the New York legislature repealed part of the expanded Married Woman's Property Act. Women could no longer share custody of their children. The setback so upset Anthony that she returned to her family farm to once again find her focus and drive.

In March 1862, President Lincoln decided that, to save the Union, he had to end slavery. He came up with a plan that called for a gradual emancipation of the slaves, beginning in the border states that had not seceded from the Union. (Eleven states had seceded, forming the Confederate States of America.) Under this plan, it would take 30 years for all slaves in the United States to be freed. Anthony was not impressed. She went out and spoke against Lincoln's plan. She believed in immediate emancipation. Her opposition asked what would be done with slaves if they were emancipated. She looked her audience in the eye when she responded:

What will the black man do with himself, is a question for him to answer. I am yet to learn that the Saxon man is the great reservoir of human rights to be doled out at his discretion to the nations of the earth. 'What will you do with the Negroes?' Do with them precisely what you do with the Irish, the Scotch, and the Germans—Educate them. Welcome them to all the blessings of our free institutions, to our schools and churches, to every department of industry, trade and art. 'Do with the Negroes?'

President Abraham Lincoln signs the Emancipation Proclamation, which freed slaves in the rebel states. Susan B.
Anthony and other abolitionists pushed to have all slaves
freed immediately and supported a constitutional amendment
outlawing slavery.

What arrogance in us to put the question, what shall
we do with a race of men and women who have fed,
clothed and supported both themselves and their
oppressors for centuries.[2]

By July, Lincoln had to rethink his plan. The border states were ignoring Lincoln's plan of gradual emancipation. So on July 13, 1862, President Lincoln announced the Emancipation Proclamation. This would go into effect on January 1, 1863, at which time all slaves in rebel states would be freed. But still, the slaves in the border states would not be freed. Abolitionists were unsatisfied. They wanted *all* slaves freed at once, and they wanted their rights protected by the Constitution.

WOMEN'S NATIONAL LOYAL LEAGUE

In March 1863, Anthony and Elizabeth Cady Stanton, along with Lucy Stone, took action against Lincoln's proclamation by organizing the Women's National Loyal League to petition for an amendment to the Constitution to outlaw slavery. Anthony nominated Stanton to be president of the league; Anthony was secretary. When Anthony addressed the first meeting of the Women's National Loyal League, she said, "Great care has been taken, ever since the war began, to keep the Negro and slavery out of sight and hearing. But my position has ever been, that instead of suppressing the real cause of the war, it should have been proclaimed, not only by the people, but by the President, Congress, Cabinet, and every military commander. And when the Government, military and civil, and the people, acknowledged slavery to be the cause of the war, they should have simultaneously, one and all, decreed its total overthrow."[3]

Following the first meeting, Anthony and other league members rallied 2,000 volunteers to help spread their message and try to gain one million signatures for a petition insisting on the complete abolition of slavery. One year after the league had formed, membership had grown to 5,000. They had succeeded in obtaining nearly 400,000 signatures. Biographers Geoffrey Ward and Ken Burns note that "the petition campaign had been the largest in history up to that time, and Senator [Charles] Sumner lavished praise on the women who had labored so hard to rally the North for freedom."[4] At last, on January 31, 1865, the

LUCY STONE

Lucy Stone was born in Massachusetts in 1818, just two years before Susan B. Anthony's birth. After Stone received her primary education, she decided she wanted to continue her education. Her father would not pay for it. So Stone accepted teaching positions to earn money to pay for her own schooling. When she was 25 years old, Stone had enough money to enroll in Oberlin College in Ohio. It was the first college to admit women and blacks. Stone remained there for four years. Upon graduation, she became the first woman from Massachusetts to receive a college degree.

Stone quickly became a strong abolitionist and women's rights leader. She spent her time touring the country and giving speeches on both topics. She spoke with sincerity and conviction. In 1853, Lucy Stone met abolitionist Henry Blackwell. They dated for two years and then married. Stone did not want marriage to take away her identity or her name; Blackwell agreed. Lucy Stone became the first woman in the United States to keep her maiden name after marriage.

Susan B. Anthony became fast friends with Lucy Stone. Anthony was impressed with her courage and her speaking abilities. Anthony once read part of Stone's speech from the 1850 Woman's Rights Convention in a newspaper and is said to have been so moved that she decided to dedicate her energies to the women's movement.

Susan B. Anthony, Elizabeth Cady Stanton, and Lucy Stone *(above)* formed the Women's National Loyal League in 1863. Like Anthony, Stone was a fervent abolitionist and women's rights leader. By the end of the decade, however, the women's movement would see a split, with Anthony and Stanton on one side and Stone on the other.

Thirteenth Amendment was proposed. It would take until December 6, 1865, for the Thirteenth Amendment to be ratified by the states. Slavery was abolished in the United States of America. The slaves were free.

Sadly, Anthony's father died during the Civil War in November 1862, due to a stomach ailment. Anthony happened to be home at the time for a short visit between lecturing. The two had been sitting together reading and discussing *The Liberator* and *Anti-Slavery Standard* when Daniel was overcome by stomach pains. Anthony and her mother helped him to bed, where he remained for two weeks before dying. He was 69 years old. Daniel Anthony had been a strong influence and supporter in Susan's life. He had taught her that men and women deserved to be treated equally. He had taught her to expect and fight for the respect that she, as a person, deserved. Susan made the funeral arrangements. The Reverend Samuel May conducted the funeral services, and Frederick Douglass paid Daniel Anthony tribute.

As the Civil War was coming to an end, Anthony decided to take an extended trip to Kansas to visit her brother, Daniel, whom their family had come to call "D.R." Anthony started off by train in January 1865. After reaching Kansas, she stayed for eight months. D.R. owned and edited

IN HER OWN WORDS

During an interview with Nellie Bly that appeared in the February 2, 1896, edition of New York *World*, Anthony was asked: "Do you ever lose hope?" As related in Lynn Sherr's *Failure Is Impossible*, Anthony responded candidly:

> Never! ... I know God never made a woman to be bossed by a man. You know [President Abraham] Lincoln said, "God never made a man good enough to govern other men without their consent." I said, "God never made a man good enough to govern any woman without her consent."

a newspaper there. During her time in Kansas, Anthony lectured throughout the state on the equality of African Americans. She also helped programs that gave aid to newly freed slaves.

Then Anthony found out that a new amendment had been proposed to the U.S. House of Representatives. The Fourteenth Amendment would give *male* citizens over the age of 21 the right to vote. Nowhere else in the Constitution had the word "male" ever appeared. Stanton wrote to Gerrit Smith, "If that word 'male' be inserted as now proposed, it will take us a century to get it out again."[5] That distinction would be disastrous to the women's movement. Anthony quickly returned to New York. She had work to do.

Anthony immediately met up with Stanton, who filled Anthony in on what had been going on while she was in Kansas. Garrison had thought there was no need for the Anti-Slavery Society once emancipation of slaves had been granted. Wendell Phillips, however, felt that the society was needed to push for extending the vote to the freed slaves. When the Anti-Slavery Society had met in May, Garrison had stepped down as president and Phillips had stepped in.

Phillips quickly made it known that he thought it was too much to hope for the granting of voting rights for both African Americans and women. Phillips suggested that it was best to try to obtain voting rights for freed African American men—a stance that became known as the "Negro's Hour" (and to Anthony as the "Negro *Man's* Hour). Stanton and Anthony could not believe it. Even Frederick Douglass, who had delivered Daniel Anthony's eulogy and had been a close family friend, supported the "Negro's Hour." Stanton wrote to Phillips, "May I ask just one question based on the apparent opposition in which you place the Negro and the woman? ... My question is this: Do you believe the African race is composed entirely of males?"[6] And Anthony told

Phillips, "I would sooner cut off my right hand ... than ask the ballot for the black man and not the woman."[7]

TAKING ACTION

One of the first tasks that Anthony did upon returning to New York was to organize a National Woman's Rights Convention for May 1866. It had been six years since the last Woman's Rights Convention. Anthony wanted to get the word out that action needed to be taken to change the wording of the proposed Fourteenth Amendment.

In addition, Anthony, along with Elizabeth Cady Stanton, Lucretia Mott, and Lucy Stone, worked to establish the American Equal Rights Association (AERA) in order to establish equal rights for *all* people—regardless of race or gender. While in the past, African-American women had been included in membership to certain women's rights committees, AERA appointed African-American women to essential management roles in the organization. African Americans Hattie Purvis and Frances Harper both served on the finance committee.

From the thousands of letters they received, Anthony and Stanton sometimes felt that they were the only people in the nation who saw the proposed wording of the Fourteenth Amendment as offensive. People who had at one time been fighting alongside Anthony and Stanton were now fighting against them. Stanton responded to one letter by saying, "With three bills before Congress to exclude [women] from all hope of representation in the future, I thank God that two women of the nation felt the insult and decided to rouse the rest to use the only right we have in the government—the right of petition. If the petition goes with our names alone, ours be the glory, and the disgrace to all the rest! ... When your granddaughters hear that against such insults you made no protest, they will blush for their ancestry."[8] Yet despite Anthony and Stanton's efforts,

Congress passed the Fourteenth Amendment soon after the AERA was formed—with no change to its wording. The amendment would now go to states to be ratified, which it was on July 9, 1868.

By May 1867, Anthony was already preparing for the first-anniversary meeting of the AERA. And Anthony had found a supporter for women's suffrage in Sojourner Truth. Anthony had the 70-year-old former slave speak at the meeting. Truth said, "There is a great stir about colored men getting their rights, but not a word about the colored women; and if colored men get their rights, and not colored women theirs, you see the colored men will be masters over the women, and it will be just as bad as it was before."[9] Anthony hoped that Truth's words reached the delegates and that together they could gain support for women's suffrage.

Anthony and Stanton were eager to participate in New York's constitutional convention in June. They put all their energies into gathering signatures of women petitioning to gain the vote. Anthony even got the help of Mrs. Horace Greeley, the wife of a prominent figure against women's suffrage who would be speaking at the convention. Anthony would not be allowed to present the petitions in person during the constitutional convention, so she asked George William Curtis to do so. On the day of the convention, Curtis was ready with the petitions. After introductions were made, Curtis rose and said, "Mr. President, I hold in my hand a petition from Mrs. Horace Greeley and three hundred other women citizens of Westchester, asking that the word 'male' by stricken from the Constitution."[10] Horace Greeley was shocked. He would later tell Anthony and Stanton that "you two ladies are the most maneuvering politicians in the State of New York. You set out to annoy me in the Constitutional Convention and you did it effectually. I saw in the manner my wife's petition was presented,

Magee, 316 Chesnut S.t Phil.ª

GEORGE F. TRAIN.

While fighting for women's suffrage in Kansas in 1867, Susan B. Anthony and Elizabeth Cady Stanton formed an unlikely alliance with George F. Train. He was a racist who had supported the South in the Civil War, but he was also a millionaire who believed in women's rights. Others in the women's movement condemned the relationship.

that Mr. Curtis was acting under instructions. I saw the reporters prick up their ears and knew that my report and Mrs. Greeley's petition would come out together, with large headings in the city papers."[11] Still, the petition was not enough. The word "male" would stay.

Meanwhile, Lucy Stone and Henry Blackwell had spent the past few months pushing for women's suffrage in Kansas. This would be the first time in history that men would be casting ballots for women's suffrage and for blacks. When Anthony and Stanton failed to gain women's suffrage in New York, they packed their bags and headed to Kansas in July.

The prospects were not looking good for women's suffrage in Kansas. Republicans and abolitionists alike were unwilling to campaign for the rights of women. In addition, Anthony and Stanton found it difficult to raise funds for the campaign, and blacks feared that they would lose their vote if they included women. Anthony and Stanton felt betrayed and alone.

As a result of Anthony and Stanton's desperation, they struck up an unlikely relationship. It was with a man named George Francis Train. Train lived in the North but supported the South. He was a Democrat and an outspoken racist. He was also a millionaire with political ambitions—a politician who believed in women's rights. Train offered Stanton and Anthony the money needed to push forward with their campaign for the women's vote. The desperate women agreed.

THE REVOLUTION

Train arrived in Kansas at his own expense, and he and Anthony began to make speeches together across the state. Anthony would begin the speeches, and then Train would carry on, often making blatant racist remarks toward African Americans. He even made rude comments to the audience about Anthony herself. Yet, no matter how crude or racist Train's comments became, Anthony held her tongue and did not defend herself or African Americans. She had agreed to Train's financial support for the women's cause. As long as Train continued to speak in favor of women's voting rights, she overlooked his extreme bigotry.

Despite the financial support from Train, women—and blacks—were unable to gain voting rights in Kansas. Anthony and the others tried to look at the situation in a positive light. Olympia Brown noted, "With all the obstacles which the dominant party could throw in our way; without organization, without money, without political rewards to offer, we gained one-third of all the votes! Surely it was a great triumph of principle."[12]

In addition to the speeches, Train helped Anthony and Stanton begin a newspaper, which Train hoped could serve both their purposes—for himself, to give him a political edge; and for Anthony and Stanton, to give them a place to write about women's rights. Stanton and Anthony decided to take Train up on his offer.

Many of Anthony and Stanton's closest friends could not accept their decision to team up with Train. Lucy Stone was especially distressed by the women's association with him. Stone wrote, "We are now in the midst of a serious quarrel with Miss Anthony and Mrs. Stanton and the Train admixture."[13] This was the beginning of a falling out between Stone and Anthony. And along with the strained friendship came a split in the suffrage movement, which hindered the movement's effectiveness.

Despite Stone's concern with what Anthony and Stanton were doing, *The Revolution* began publication in New York in 1868, with the debut paper appearing on newsstands on January 8. When the offices opened, there were portraits of Lucretia Mott and Mary Wollstonecraft, two early leaders in the women's rights movement, on the walls. The weekly paper's motto read, "Men their rights and nothing more, women their rights and nothing less."[14] The newspaper campaigned for equal rights for all American citizens, including former slaves. Anthony and Stanton also advocated for an eight-hour workday and equal pay for equal work.

By the fall, Anthony had formed the Working Women's Association, in order to create an organization in which working women could find support from other working women. Through this association, Anthony talked to working women and then wrote reports on their working and living conditions. At one meeting, Anthony told them, "You must not work for these starving prices any longer. Talk to one another, and I will come and talk to you, and the press will support you, and by and by we will have an immense mass meeting of women, where all can talk if they choose, and all the good men and women of America, listening to your appeal will come forward and stand by you."[15]

Anthony used the newspaper to speak out about the proposed Fifteenth Amendment, which would prevent states from stopping people from voting on the basis of race or color. The Fifteenth Amendment said nothing of women. Anthony felt that the amendment did not offer equality to everyone.

At the annual meeting of the AERA in May 1869, Anthony told listeners, "[The Fifteenth Amendment would] put 2,000,000 colored men in the position of tyrants over 2,000,000 colored women, who until now had at least been the equals to the men at their side."[16] She also said that "[women's suffrage] will place [every woman] in a position in which she can earn her own bread, so that she can go out into the world on equal competition in the struggle for life, so that she shall not be compelled to take such positions as men choose to accord her ... and then take such pay as men choose to give her."[17] Congress had approved the wording of the Fifteenth Amendment one month before the AERA meeting, and it would be ratified by the states on February 3, 1870. Anthony and Stanton hoped for a Sixteenth Amendment that would give women the right to vote.

DIVISIONS IN THE MOVEMENT

Anthony and Stanton were finding themselves at odds with many members of the AERA. The split over the support in the Fifteenth Amendment had intensified, which became apparent at the May 1869 meeting. The opposition between AERA members had made the organization weaker and less productive. While the majority of AERA members believed the Fifteenth Amendment to be good for the movement, as it brought people one step closer to the ultimate goal—obtaining equality for all people—Stanton and Anthony disagreed. They saw it as a step backward in allowing uneducated black men the opportunity to vote ahead of educated white women. As a result of their beliefs, Anthony and Stanton disassociated themselves from the AERA.

Instead, Anthony and Stanton formed the National Woman Suffrage Association (NWSA) in 1869, of which Stanton was chosen president. The women decided that they would not allow any man to hold an office in the association. The association's plan was to address the rights of women. The NWSA believed that the Fourteenth and Fifteenth amendments were unjust to women. The association worked to make it easier for women to obtain divorces. It wanted equal employment and pay for men and women. It wanted an eight-hour workday. To obtain these rights, Anthony and Stanton felt it was necessary to gain a federal amendment to the Constitution stating these rights.

Lucy Stone, who did believe in the Fourteenth and Fifteenth amendments and had organized the New England

A crowd of women joining the National Woman Suffrage Association is seen in this illustration from 1869. That year, as divisions were roiling the women's movement, Susan B. Anthony and Elizabeth Cady Stanton organized the NWSA. A second group, the American Woman Suffrage Association, was founded by Lucy Stone.

Woman Suffrage Association, decided to create the American Woman Suffrage Association (AWSA). She stated, "I think we need two national associations for woman suffrage ... so that those who do not oppose the Fifteenth Amendment, or take the tone of *The Revolution*, may yet have an organization with which they can work in harmony."[18] The Reverend Henry Ward Beecher, a prominent clergyman and social reformer, became the AWSA president. To further show her unhappiness with and separation from Anthony and Stanton, Stone launched her own newspaper called *The Woman's Journal*, which made its debut on January 8, 1870—the second anniversary of *The Revolution*.

By the spring of 1870, it had become clear that the competition *The Woman's Journal* brought to *The Revolution* was taking away subscriptions. In addition, *The Revolution* had lost the financial support of Train, who had stopped giving money almost as soon as it became established. Other financial supporters, like sisters Harriet Beecher Stowe and Isabella Beecher Hooker, withdrew an offer to support the newspaper when Anthony and Stanton refused to consider a name change for *The Revolution*. Although Anthony tried desperately to save the newspaper she had helped start—including using her savings, borrowing money from friends and family, and raising subscription prices—she finally realized she would have to sell the paper. She sold it to Laura Curtis Bullard and Theodore Tilton. Much to Anthony's dismay, they turned the paper into a literary and society journal. Adding to Anthony's depression was the debt she had accumulated over the previous two years to keep the newspaper afloat. Anthony was now responsible for a personal debt of $10,000. She refused to declare bankruptcy, vowing to pay back all the money when able.

A Tower
of Strength

Susan B. Anthony's desire to spread the word about women's issues took her all over the country. She traveled by train, horse, streetcar, ship, wagon, and boat. Sometimes she went weeks and even months living out of hotels and taverns. In her diary she wrote, "I have been on tours for four months, sometimes without the luxury of a cup of coffee in a private home. Once I was traveling for six months without a home-cooked meal. One gets very tired of mediocre hotels and stage depot dining rooms."[1]

Newspapers reported on Anthony's stage presence and speaking abilities. One paper wrote, "Miss Anthony evidently lectures not for the purpose of receiving applause, but for the purpose of making people understand and be convinced. She takes her position on the stage in a plain and unassuming manner and speaks extemporaneously and fluently, too, reminding one of an old campaign speaker, who is accustomed to talk simply for the purpose of converting his audience to his political theories. She used plain English and plenty of it. ... She clearly evinced a quality that many politicians lack—sincerity."[2] Susan B. Anthony was making an impression wherever she went. She was easy to understand, she made herself heard, and she got her audience to think.

In a letter she wrote in 1871, Anthony described the terrible roads she encountered: "I am now over one hundred miles on my stage-route south, and horrible indeed are the roads—miles and miles of corduroy"—logs laid across the mud—"and then twenty miles of 'Joe Lane black mud,' as they call it, because old Joseph Lane settled right here in the midst of it. It is heavy clay without a particle of loam and rolls up on the wheels until rim, spokes and hub are one solid circle. The wheels cease to turn and actually slide over the ground, and then driver and men passengers jump out and with chisels and shingles cut the clay off the wheels."[3] Yet Anthony let nothing stop her. She readily put up with the discomforts of her travels in order to spread the word for suffrage.

In 1869, Anthony called for the first Woman Suffrage Convention in Washington, D.C. This gathering of NWSA members would be repeated twice a year for years to come to educate members on the importance of the vote. One reporter remarked of Anthony's dedication and influence on the meeting: "Miss Anthony is the ruling spirit of the convention. She dominates. She is constantly on the alert and has a keen appreciation of every point made by a speaker. She lets no point pass without emphasizing it and impressing it upon the convention. She talks a great deal, but never without having something to say. From the woman suffrage standpoint she is a tower of strength."[4]

HALF A CENTURY STRONG

On February 15, 1870, Susan B. Anthony turned 50 years old. Some women of the time lied about their age, wanting to remain young in the eyes of the public. Anthony, however, embraced this landmark birthday. She got together with numerous close friends at the Women's Bureau in New York City, where they celebrated with cake, presents, and poetry. In Anthony's diary, she wrote, "Fiftieth birthday! One half-century done, one score of it hard labor for bettering humanity—temperance—emancipation—enfranchisement—oh, such a struggle!"[5]

Unfortunately, Guelma and Hannah could not attend the celebration, as they were busy with their families. Anthony's mother, Lucy, was too frail to travel. Elizabeth Cady Stanton also could not attend, as she was ill. Still, Anthony was touched by those who came. When it was her turn to talk after listening to the telegrams, poems, and testimonials, Anthony found herself momentarily at a loss for words. Looking out at the audience, she confessed, "I never made a speech except to rouse people to action."[6] Perhaps those spoken words prompted her to do just that: rouse her audience to action. She would later tell her guests, "I ask you tonight, as your best testimony of my services, on this, the twentieth anniversary of my public work, to join me in making a demand on Congress for a Sixteenth Amendment giving women the right to vote, and then to go with me before the several legislatures to secure its ratification; and when the Secretary of State proclaims that that amendment has been ratified by the twenty-eight states, then Susan B. Anthony will stop work—but not before."[7]

Yet it was soon after her birthday that Anthony lost the newspaper, *The Revolution*, and she was feeling down and discouraged. In addition, Stanton had stopped attending nearly all the conventions. Anthony was dismayed when Stanton failed to appear at the national convention in

January 1871. She told Stanton, "How you can excuse your-self is more than I can understand."[8] Instead of attending conventions, Stanton was busy earning money for her fam-ily because Stanton's husband could not cover the cost of their children's college tuition on his own. Stanton earned the money by giving lectures on women's rights. Still, Anthony saw Stanton's failure to attend the conventions as irresponsible to the women's cause.

It was at this 1871 National Convention that Anthony invited a controversial women's rights activist, Victoria Woodhull, to speak. What made Woodhull controversial was the fact that she was divorced and promoted "free love," which meant having relationships out of wedlock. Anthony did not care about Woodhull's views on relationships—what interested her were Woodhull's views on women's suf-frage. Anthony had just heard her address a committee of Congress—the first woman to do so. Woodhull believed women already had the right to vote under the Fourteenth and Fifteenth amendments. She wanted Congress to pass an act that would guarantee women's rights. Woodhull told the committee members, "The Constitution defines a woman born or naturalized in the United States, and subject to the jurisdiction thereof, to be a citizen. It recognizes the right of a citizen to vote. It declares that the right of a citizen to vote shall not be denied or abridged by the United States or any state on the account of 'race, color, or previous condi-tion of servitude.'"[9] Anthony was so taken with her speech that she asked her to repeat it for the National Convention later that afternoon.

In June of that year, Stanton did agree to go on a trip from Chicago to California with Anthony. Anthony had already been on the road for months, making speeches and working to raise awareness of the women's rights move-ment. Anthony welcomed Stanton's company. Anthony, tall and lean with a stern look about her, and Stanton, short

Victoria Woodhull reads her argument in favor of women's suffrage in 1871 before the Judiciary Committee of the House of Representatives. She was the first woman ever to address a committee of Congress. Anthony invited her to repeat her speech at the convention of the National Woman Suffrage Association.

and round with a motherly look about her, made a noticeable pair. The two women took the train and stopped and lectured in various cities about women's rights.

It would be Anthony's first trip to California, and the two friends took time to visit Yosemite Valley. Anthony describes the scenery in a letter she wrote during her trip: "I went up the Mariposa trail [on horseback] seven miles to Artist's Point, and there under a big pine tree, on a rock jutting out over the valley, sat and gazed at the wondrous walls with their peaks and spires and domes"[10] The day before the two women had gone out together, but Stanton had worn herself out with the day's horseback riding. So while Anthony explored the Mariposa trail, Stanton remained in bed.

Unfortunately, Stanton's trip was cut short when her mother fell ill and Stanton had to return east to be with her. Anthony did not turn back, however, and continued on to Oregon and Washington without her friend. Anthony estimated that she had traveled 13,000 miles (20,921 kilometers) during 1871. From January to June, she had given 63 lectures; she gave another 26 as she made her way to California, and another 82 in Oregon and Washington.

In 1872, Anthony's connection to Woodhull would cause a scandal for the women's movement. Woodhull used the National Woman Suffrage Association to announce a new political party called the People's Party. Woodhull also planned to run for president of the United States. Anthony was not pleased; her associations were not to be used for political campaigns—they were strictly for gaining women's suffrage. She quickly cut off her relationship with Woodhull. Anthony later noted in her diary, "There was never such a foolish muddle. … Our movement as such is so demoralized by the letting go of the helm of the ship to Woodhull— though we rescued it—It was by a hair breadth escape."[11]

VOTING FOR PRESIDENT

As Woodhull and others had done, Anthony took the position that the Fourteenth Amendment gave women the right to vote in federal elections. Anthony had been planning to vote for some time—she just needed to be home instead of traveling. New York law required voters to reside in the district in which they voted for 30 days before an election. In 1872, Anthony would get her chance.

On November 1, 1872, the Anthony sisters—Guelma, Susan, Hannah, and Mary—arrived at a barbershop in Rochester, New York, to register to vote. The registrars were unsure about allowing the women to register at first, but they eventually allowed the four women, along with 12 other women, to register. A few days later, the women returned to officially vote in a presidential election. It would be the only time Susan B. Anthony placed a vote for president of the United States.

Then on Thanksgiving Day, a United States marshal arrived at Anthony's home to place her under arrest for her vote. The marshal and Anthony rode a horse-drawn trolley downtown. When the trolley driver asked Anthony for her fare, Anthony told him, "I am traveling at the expense of the government. … Ask him for my fare."[12] Anthony then pointed to the United States marshal.

Anthony and the other women who had voted all had their bail set at $500. All the women paid their bail—all except for Anthony. She wanted her case taken to the Supreme Court. When she refused to pay, her bail was reissued at $1,000. Still she refused. But then her attorney, Henry Selden, paid Anthony's bail out of his own pocket. By doing so, Anthony lost her chance to take her case to the Supreme Court. She was devastated. When an upset Anthony asked Selden if he realized what he had done by posting bail, he responded, "Yes … but I could not see a lady I respected put in jail."[13]

Until her trial in June, Anthony continued her life as usual, traveling around to give her speech entitled "Is It a Crime for a Citizen of the United States to Vote?" When her trial finally began on June 17, 1873, Anthony stood in front of Judge Ward Hunt, who told Anthony that she could not testify on her own behalf because "women were incompetent to do so."[14] After Hunt told the jury to find Anthony guilty as charged, he asked Anthony if she had anything she wanted to say. She did: "Yes, your honor, I have many things to say; for in your ordered verdict of guilty you have trampled under foot every vital principle of our government. My natural rights, my civil rights, my political rights, my judicial rights are all alike ignored. Robbed of the fundamental privilege of citizenship, I am

This cartoon of Susan B. Anthony appeared on the cover of *The Daily Graphic* on June 5, 1873, just before she went on trial for voting in the presidential election of 1872. The illustration was captioned "The Woman Who Dared." The women in the background are campaigning for equality.

degraded from the status of a citizen to that of a subject; and not only myself individually but all of my sex are, by your honor's verdict, doomed to political subjection under this so-called republican form of government."[15]

Judge Hunt fined Anthony $100, which she never paid. Another woman, Virginia Minor, had also tried to register to vote in the 1872 election. Unlike Anthony, however, Minor was not allowed to register. Minor and her husband sued the registrar, Reese Happersett, for denying her that right. Minor's case went all the way to the Supreme Court in 1874, but the justices voted unanimously in favor of Happersett. They decided that citizenship alone did not grant women the right to vote but that each individual state could decide if a woman had the right to vote. Anthony was not pleased: "If we once establish the false principle that United States citizenship does not carry with it the right to vote in every state in this union, there is no end to the petty freaks and cunning devices that [will] be resorted to exclude one and another class of citizens from the right of suffrage."[16] Anthony and Stanton believed that now, more than ever, they must work toward a women's-suffrage amendment to the Constitution.

THE CENTENNIAL EXHIBITION

In 1876, 100 years after the birth of the United States, Anthony and Stanton felt that women had made little progress in gaining equal rights to men. The two friends feared that it would take another 100 years for women to gain these rights. Still, they did not lose hope. They decided to turn their attentions to Philadelphia and partake in the Centennial Exhibition. While in Philadelphia, Anthony and Stanton teamed up with Matilda Joslyn Gage to write a new Declaration of Rights for Women. They wrote, "We protest against this government of the United States as an oligarchy of sex, and not a true republic; and we protest

LIVING SINGLE

Being a single woman in Susan B. Anthony's time meant being labeled an "old maid." Society looked at single women as outcasts. Society expected single women to live with married relatives; it was not appropriate for a single woman to have a home of her own. Anthony did not agree. She wrote a speech on the topic entitled "The Homes of Single Women." In her speech, she told her audiences, "A Home of one's own is the want, the necessity of every human being, the one thing above all others longed for, worked for. Whether the humblest cottage or the proudest palace, a home of our own is the soul's dream of rest, the one hope that will not die until we have reached the very portals of the everlasting home."*

Anthony never had a home of her own. She spent much of her time traveling for her work. Between lectures, when she wanted some down time, she would stay with family—her parents when they were alive, her sister Guelma, her brother Daniel, or her sister Hannah. Eventually, she and her single sister, Mary, both lived at their family's home in Rochester, New York.

While Anthony may have longed for a home, she did not have to long for her freedom and independence. Being single allowed her to make her own decisions and handle her own money. When she saw other single women living happy and content lives without husbands, she saw that "as young women become educated in the industries of the world, thereby learning the sweetness of independent bread, it will be more and more impossible for them to accept the Blackstone marriage limitation that 'husband and wife are one, and that the one is the husband.'"**

---

*Kathleen Barry, *Susan B. Anthony: A Biography of a Singular Feminist.* New York: Ballantine Books, 1988, p. 261.
**Ibid., p. 261.

against calling this a centennial celebration of the indepen-dence of the United States."[17]

Stanton worked hard to try to get their Declaration included in the official Fourth of July ceremony, but the program had already been set and those in charge were not willing to make changes so close to the day. When she pressed the president of the Centennial Commission, General Joseph Roswell Hawley, Stanton was given the same answer. There was no way to include the Declaration, nor was there any way for Stanton and the other National Woman Suffrage Association leaders to get a seat at the ceremony. Hawley finally told Stanton, "We propose to cel-ebrate what we have done the last hundred years, not what we have failed to do."[18]

Anthony, however, had no plans of missing the ceremony. Her brother Daniel (D.R.) ran a newspaper in Kansas, and he let Anthony use his press pass to obtain a seat at the ceremony. She was able to finagle four more seats. Stanton, however, was so upset with Hawley, she no longer wanted to attend. She arranged for a women's rights meeting to be held at the same time as the ceremony. Anthony appreciated Stanton's feelings, but Anthony still went to the ceremony. She gave the other four tickets to coworkers.

At the ceremony on July 4, 1876, Anthony and her four friends listened as Richard Henry Lee, a descendant of one of the signers, read the Declaration of Independence to the audience. When Lee read the words "our sacred honor,"[19] Anthony rose from her seat and walked to the front of the stage, with her four coworkers following her. When Anthony reached the stage, she handed a rolled-up copy of the Declaration of Rights for Women, tied with a ribbon, to Thomas Ferry, the acting vice president of the United States, who was standing at the podium. When Ferry accepted the document, the five women turned and walked away. As they made their way back up the aisle, the four coworkers passed out copies of the declaration to any person with an outstretched arm. The women walked out of the Independence Hall to a bandstand set up in Independence Square, where Anthony read the Declaration of Rights for Women to a gathering crowd.

WRITING AND WORD CHOICES

Soon after this, Anthony, Stanton, and Gage got to work writing a four-volume set of books entitled *History of Woman Suffrage*. Volume I came out in 1881 followed by Volumes II, III, and IV in 1882, 1885, and 1902, respectively. Anthony and Stanton spent long hours together during this time at Stanton's home in Tenafly, New Jersey. The two found themselves forced to relive painful memories, which sometimes brought about bickering and hurt feelings. But at the day's end, they had made up; their friendship always prevailed. Margaret, Stanton's oldest daughter, observed that:

> Susan is punctilious on dates, mother on philosophy, but each contends as stoutly in the other's domain as if equally strong on both points. Sometimes these disputes run so high that down go the pens, one sails out one door and one out the other, walking in opposite directions around the estate and just as I have made up my mind that this beautiful friendship of forty years has at last terminated, I see them walking down the hill, arm in arm. ... When they return they go straight to work where they left off, as if nothing had ever happened. ... The one that was unquestionably right assumes it, and the other silently concedes the fact. They never explain, nor apologize, nor shed tears, nor make up, as other people do.[20]

Susan B. Anthony *(left)* and Elizabeth Cady Stanton, along with Matilda Joslyn Gage, worked together to write the four-volume *History of Woman Suffrage*. The first volume was published in 1881; the final, in 1902. Anthony did not relish writing, saying in her diary: "I love to make history but hate to write it."

Anthony, while she believed in the work they were doing and understood its importance, was not a fan of writing. She noted in her diary, "I love to make history but hate to write it." [21]

On January 10, 1878, a newly worded Sixteenth Amendment to the Constitution was introduced in the Senate by Senator Arlen A. Sargent of California. The amendment read, "The right of citizens to vote shall not be denied or abridged by the United States or any State on account of sex."[22] The amendment did not make it out of the Senate Committee on Privileges and Elections. Anthony put the pressure on. She started to spend more time in Washington, getting to know the representatives and senators. She made speeches and met with the press. People came to recognize her trademark red shawl, which she wore nearly every time she spoke in public. Each winter, Anthony held the National Woman Suffrage Association convention in Washington. Her presence was felt, and she became the symbol of women's suffrage.

Meanwhile, Stanton was busy working on their books, with the help of her daughter, Harriot. Stanton continued to do less and less convention work, leaving Anthony with that task. When Stanton and her daughter had finished proofreading the second book, Stanton went to live in Europe, part of the time with her son Theodore and the other part with Harriot, and their families. During this time, Anthony and Stanton stayed in touch through letters, but they rarely saw each other during the next 10 years.

On January 23, 1880, Anthony stood before the Committee on the Judiciary in the United States Senate to give a speech entitled "On Behalf of the Woman Suffrage Amendment." Early in her speech, she noted, "We women have been standing before the American republic for thirty years, asking the men to take yet one step further and extend the practical application of the theory of equality of rights to all the people to the other half of the people—the women. That is all that I stand here to-day to attempt to demand."[23]

In 1880, Susan B. Anthony's mother, Lucy, died. The past decade had been a difficult time for Anthony. She had seen Guelma die in 1873 and Hannah die in 1877. Guelma had contracted tuberculosis, leaving her weak and suffering

IN HER OWN WORDS

During a speech in 1888, as recounted in Lynn Sherr's *Failure Is Impossible*, Susan B. Anthony explained why women deserved the vote:

> What is this little thing that we are asking for? It seems so little; it is yet everything. ... What does your right to vote in this country, men and brethren, say to you? What does that right say to every possible man, native and foreign, black and white, rich and poor, educated and ignorant, drunk and sober, to every possible man outside the State prison, the idiot and the lunatic asylums? What does it everywhere under the shadow of the American flag say to every man? It says, "Your judgment is sound, your opinion is worthy to be counted." That is it. And now, on the other hand, what does it say to every possible woman, native and foreign, black and white, rich and poor, educated and ignorant, virtuous and vicious, to every possible woman under the shadow of our flag? It says, "Your judgment is not sound, your opinion is not worthy to be counted." ... [Women] shall stand and plead and demand the right to be heard, and not only to be heard, but to have our votes counted and coined into law, until the very crack of doom, if need be.

during her final months. Then Susan had rushed out West to be with Hannah when she died of the same disease. Although Anthony spent much of her life on the road and away from home, she felt a deep connection with her family and each death was painful and hard on her. What kept Anthony going was throwing herself back into her work, just as she had when her father died during the Civil War.

But first, Anthony would go on a nine-month voyage farther than she had ever traveled—she went to Europe, visiting England, Ireland, and France. She left in early 1883 and did not come home until November. She spent some of her days acting like a true tourist, taking in the sights. Other days, she spent time with Stanton in London and with Stanton's son, Theodore, who lived with his family in Paris. And of course, Anthony took time to meet with influential women leaders.

DUELING ASSOCIATIONS

In 1887, for the first time, the full Senate would vote on the women's-suffrage amendment. It lost 34 to 16. Still, it was a breakthrough for the movement that the amendment had made it to the Senate floor for a vote. Suddenly, it seemed more important than ever to get women out there campaigning and working toward suffrage.

During the 1880s, the American Woman Suffrage Association, led by Lucy Stone, was making news. Although the group had the same agenda as the National Woman Suffrage Association—obtaining women's suffrage—it took a different approach. Stone believed there to be a faster way to women's suffrage than an amendment to the Constitution. She wanted to see each state take on women's suffrage. She also believed that accepting partial suffrage would be adequate, meaning she would accept women having the right to vote on particular issues, such as education.

Anthony, however, disagreed entirely with Stone's position. In her speech entitled "On Behalf of the Woman Suffrage Amendment," Anthony noted:

> Then you ask why we do not get suffrage by the popular-vote method, State by State? I answer, because there is no reason why I, for instance, should desire the women of one State of this nation to vote any more than the women of another State.

DID YOU KNOW?

Not only did Susan B. Anthony want to acknowledge equality between the sexes in the United States, she also wanted to see equality across the world. In 1887, she began work to set up the International Council of Women. The following year, the council met for the first time in Washington, D.C., with more than 80 speakers lined up to appear at the one-week event. Representatives from England, France, Ireland, Norway, Denmark, Finland, India, Canada, and the United States were present. President Grover Cleveland and his wife, Frances, opened the event, and Anthony began the council's first session, introducing Elizabeth Cady Stanton, the first speaker. When Stanton took the platform, she said, "Whether our feet are compressed in iron shoes, our faces hidden with veils and masks; whether yoked with cows to draw the plow through its furrows, or classed with idiots, lunatics and criminals in the laws and constitutions of the State, the principle is the same; for the humiliations of spirit are as real as the visible badges of servitude."*

*Kathleen Barry, *Susan B. Anthony: A Biography of a Singular Feminist*. New York: Ballantine Books, 1988, p. 287.

A session of the National Woman Suffrage Association was held in 1880 during a political convention in Chicago. During the 1880s, the NWSA pushed for a constitutional amendment giving women the vote. The American Woman Suffrage Association sought to see states approve women's suffrage. Soon, though, the former rival groups would merge.

... The reason why I do not wish to get this right by what you call the popular-vote method, the State vote, is because I believe there is a United States citizenship. I believe that this is a nation, and to be a citizen of this nation should be a guaranty to every citizen of the right to a voice in the Government, and should give to me my right to express my opinion. You deny to me my liberty, my freedom, if you say that I shall have no voice whatever in making, shaping, or controlling the conditions of society in which I live.[24]

For years Stone and Anthony had been fighting for the same outcome, but approaching it in different ways.

In February 1890, Anthony and Stone finally laid aside their differences and helped found the National American Woman Suffrage Association (NAWSA). It was a merger of the two former rival groups, the NWSA and the AWSA. Stone's daughter, Alice Stone Blackwell, who had grown up to become an activist, initiated the merger between the two associations.

The NAWSA would focus on a national amendment to secure women the vote. However, as Sara Evans noted in her book entitled *Born for Liberty: A History of Women in America*, "Even though Anthony preferred to work for a federal amendment to the Constitution, many others continued to advocate state level pressure for referenda and legislation. Those local campaigns had the virtue of involving and educating thousands of women, as well as a new generation, and building local alliances. As a strategy, however, experience proved state campaigns to be weak indeed."[25]

Stanton told a friend, "Lucy [Stone] and Susan alike see suffrage only. They do not see woman's religious and social bondage. Neither do the young women in either association, hence they may as well combine for they have one mind and purpose."[26] Stanton became the organization's first president, after Anthony pressed the delegates to elect her. They wanted Anthony to be president, but Anthony felt that position belonged to Stanton. Anthony told them, "When the division [between the NWSA and AWSA] was made twenty-two years ago, it was because our platform was too broad, because Mrs. Stanton was too radical. A more conservative association was wanted. And now if we divide and Mrs. Stanton shall be deposed from the presidency you virtually degrade her."[27] The delegates obliged and elected Stanton as its first president; Anthony became vice president, and Stone chaired the executive committee. Anthony later served as president from 1892 to 1900.

When Stanton made her opening speech as president of the NAWSA in 1890, she made a point of calling for equality for women in all churches and in matters of divorce. She also wanted no mention of God in the Constitution of the United States and wanted no connection between church and state. She told her delegates, "We do not want to limit our platform to bare suffrage and nothing more. … Wherever a woman is wronged her voice should be heard."[28] The day after her inaugural address, Stanton left for England once again.

A New
Generation
of Women

On July 10, 1890, history was made when Wyoming became a state—with the inclusion of women on the ballot. (As a territory, Wyoming granted women the right to vote in 1869.) In Cheyenne, suffragist Theresa Jenkins led a parade and started the speeches about gaining the right to vote. Shortly before Wyoming was admitted as a state, Anthony told an interviewer where the most progress was being made for suffrage. She said, "In the West. The people there seem to be freer in mind and more ready to listen to reason than elsewhere. Wyoming is knocking at the door of the Union, and will be admitted before long. When she comes in, we shall have our first State where women are on an equality with men as electors. After the ice is once broken by that precedent, we shall find our work easier in other quarters."[1]

AUNT SUSAN AND HER NIECES

Both Susan B. Anthony, now 71 years old, and Elizabeth Cady Stanton, now 76 years old, found themselves slowing down. In August 1891, Stanton returned to the United States and purchased an apartment in Manhattan, where she lived with her widowed daughter, Margaret, and her unmarried son, Robert. Anthony moved into her parents' home in Rochester with her sister Mary. She enjoyed feeling settled, though she continued to travel the country and speak out for women's rights. Anthony was not going to let her age stand in the way of her life's calling. A new century was quickly approaching, and Anthony still planned to spend the rest of her days fighting for what she believed in most: Women's right to the vote.

As the nineteenth century was coming to a close, Anthony was getting to meet a new generation of suffragists. Anthony came to refer to these young women as her "nieces." They, in turn, called her "Aunt Susan." One of Anthony's favorite nieces early on was Rachel Foster Avery, who had much of Anthony's own drive for women's suffrage. Avery had accompanied Anthony to Europe during her visit in 1883. Avery had also assisted Anthony, along with May Wright Sewall, when Anthony was organizing the International Council of Women in 1887 and 1888. Anthony enjoyed seeing her nieces getting involved. She believed that these young women could manage the tasks at hand. She told one interviewer, "There is so much yet to be done, I see so many things I would like to do and say, but I must leave it for the younger generation. We old fighters have prepared the way, and it is easier than it was fifty years ago when I first got into the harness. The young blood, fresh with enthusiasm and with all the enlightment of the twentieth century, must carry on the work."[2]

Although a new generation of women were taking on campaigns and lecturing, Anthony could not keep herself

In the 1890s, Susan B. Anthony moved into her parents' home in Rochester, New York, with her sister Mary (left). Anthony continued to travel around the United States to speak out for women's rights. She was also working with a new generation of suffragists.

completely out of the action. She always wanted to be busy and always wanted to be getting the word out. So, she kept on with her travels. In 1894, Anthony toured New York's 60 counties to speak for women's suffrage, as the state was about to amend its constitution. Despite her tireless efforts, the amendment did not pass. Discouraged, but not defeated, she headed to Kansas, hoping to help see that state give women the right to vote. Once again, the amendment did not pass. By 1896, Anthony was in California, where she spent eight months speaking throughout the state. Prior to her campaign, Anthony was able once again to ride horseback through the Yosemite Valley as she had done with Stanton years earlier. This time, Anthony was 75 years

DID YOU KNOW?

By 1900, bicycles had become popular in the United States. More than 10 million people owned a bicycle—many being women. Gail Collins noted that "Susan B. Anthony enthused that bicycling 'did more to emancipate women than anything else in the world.'"* In a letter, Anthony wrote, "I think [the bicycle] has done a great deal to emancipate women. I stand and rejoice every time I see a woman ride by on a wheel. It gives her a feeling of freedom, self-reliance and independence. The moment she takes her seat she knows she can't get into harm while she is on her bicycle, and away she goes, the picture of free, untrammeled womanhood."**

*Gail Collins, *America's Women: 400 Years of Dolls, Drudges, Helpmates, and Heroines.* New York: HarperCollins, 2003, p. 280.
**Lynn Sherr, *Failure Is Impossible: Susan B. Anthony In Her Own Words.* New York: Random House, 1995, p. 277.

old. When the campaigning began in California, Anthony's schedule was grueling—she sometimes spoke three times a day. Yet California, too, did not pass an amendment for women's suffrage. After Wyoming, only three states would pass women's suffrage before 1900—all in the West, as Anthony had predicted. In 1893, Colorado won the vote; and in 1896, Utah and Idaho won the vote.

One issue Anthony had worked hard on over her lifetime was coeducation. And one university in particular that she wished to see admit women in her lifetime was the University of Rochester. In 1879, when David J. Hill had taken over as president, Anthony had immediately organized a group of Rochester women to demand that the university admit women, as Syracuse University and Harvard University had recently done. Hill told Anthony that coeducation was not possible for the University of Rochester at that time.

Twelve years later, in 1891, Anthony made her demand again when Hill began to seek local support for the university. Again, Hill said no. In the East, it was much more popular to have women's colleges and men's colleges (this was not true in the Midwest and West, where many colleges were now opening their doors to women). When Anthony persisted, the University of Rochester told her that $200,000 would have to be raised to admit women to the college. Apparently, that was the cost of the additional students. As that sounded out of reach to Anthony, she tried another strategy. She asked Hill to admit one woman, Helen Wilkinson, in the next school year and Anthony would pay for her expenses. Hill agreed, and Wilkinson began classes. The men on campus taunted her at first, but it soon became clear that having a woman on campus was not going to turn it upside-down. Wilkinson remained at the school for two years. She had to withdraw when she became seriously ill—an illness that took her life the following year.

In 1898, the University of Rochester lowered its monetary requirement to admit women to $100,000 and then lowered it to $50,000 the following year. By 1900, Anthony and her followers had raised $40,000. The day before the deadline to turn in the required amount, Anthony learned they were $8,000 short. She spent the day working. She asked her sister Mary, who gave her $2,000. She went door to door, stopping at stores and factories. A close friend of Anthony's, the Reverend Gannett, contributed another $2,000. Leaving Gannett, Anthony continued to knock at offices and stores until she finally had the money. She marched into the university's offices and handed it over. But the school declared that she was still short $2,000!

Anthony, tired after her long day of raising money, would not be sent home now. She said, "Well gentlemen, I may as well confess—I am the guarantor ... I now pledge my life insurance for the $2,000."[3] Susan B. Anthony had done it! She had ensured the admittance of women to the University of Rochester. Her efforts, though, did not come without a price. Just days after her hard work, Anthony suffered a stroke. She experienced some paralysis and loss of speech. She was restricted to her bed for weeks. But the moment she felt well enough, she asked to be taken to the University of Rochester. She wanted to see the women on campus, enjoying their rights to study at the college.

EVER A RADICAL

In 1895, Stanton, having just turned 80 years old, published a book entitled *The Woman's Bible*. In the past few years, Stanton had begun to shift her focus from concentrating on women's suffrage to fighting the church. Critics of the book called it obscene, considering it disrespectful to Protestantism. Even some delegates of the National American Woman Suffrage Association thought the radical Stanton had gone too far. Delegates moved to disassociate the organization from Stanton entirely. Anthony herself did not wholly agree with the ideas Stanton had presented in the book. Anthony told her, "You say 'women must be emancipated from their superstitions before enfranchisement will be of any benefit,' and I say just the reverse, that women must be enfranchised before they can be emancipated from their superstitions. … So you will have to keep pegging away, saying, 'Get rid of religious bigotry and then get political rights;' while I shall keep pegging away, saying 'Get political rights first and religious bigotry will melt like dew before morning sun;' and each will continue still to believe in and defend the other."[4]

And believe in and defend Stanton is just what Anthony did. When delegates from the National American wanted to censure Stanton, Anthony spoke on her friend's behalf by saying, "When our platform becomes too narrow for people of all creeds and of no creeds, I myself shall not stand upon it. … I shall be pained beyond expression if the delegates … are so narrow and illiberal as to adopt this resolution. You [had] better not begin resolving against individual action or you will find no limit. This year it is Mrs. Stanton; next year it may be me or one of yourselves who will be the victim."[5] Despite Anthony's efforts, the delegates voted 53 to 41 in favor of separating themselves from Stanton. Stanton asked Anthony to resign, as she had from the Women's State Temperance Society when those members had voted Stanton out of the organization. Anthony thought about whether to resign for three weeks. She was uncertain what to do. In the end, however, she decided she needed to maintain her position as president in order to guide these women. She wrote to Stanton, "… instead of my resigning and leaving those half-fledged chickens without any mother, I think it my duty, and the duty of yourself and all the liberals to be at the next convention and try to reverse this miserable narrow action."[6]

A drawing for the National American Woman Suffrage Association's convention in January 1896 depicts Elizabeth Cady Stanton, George Washington, and Susan B. Anthony. Stanton is holding a copy of *The Woman's Bible*, which some critics called obscene. Delegates in the NAWSA voted to separate the group from Stanton.

In 1897, Anthony created a workroom in her Rochester home's attic, where she and Ida Husted Harper began work on her biography. Anthony had met Harper, an Indiana reporter, the year before. The two women had instantly formed a friendship. Anthony asked Harper to come to her home to write her biography; Harper agreed. The following year, *The Life and Work of Susan B. Anthony: A Story of the Evolution of the Status of Women* was published.

PASSING THE TORCH

In 1900, Anthony made an important decision. She was going to step down from her position as president of the National American Woman Suffrage Association. She was 80 years old and had been a leader of the National American and its predecessor for the last 30 years. Anthony wanted to watch the next generation of women at work for women's suffrage so that she could be assured that the job was done correctly. She said, "I am not retiring now because I feel unable, mentally or physically, to do the necessary work, but because I wish to see the organization in the hands of those who are to have its management in the future. I want to see you all at work, while I am alive, so I can scold if you do not do it well."[7]

IN HER OWN WORDS

On December 30, 1900, an interviewer asked Susan B. Anthony, "What is the chief danger, social or political, that confronts the new century?" According to Lynn Sherr's book *Failure Is Impossible*, Anthony responded:

> The chief danger, socially and politically, that confronts the coming century lies in man's ignoring woman in the making and executing of the laws that govern the world—in man's egotism, which causes him to think he can run the government machine alone. Not until he calls to his aid the woman at his side, counting her opinion at the ballot-box in the election of every officer so that from President to policeman all must reckon with her, will the world be redeemed from the social and political corruption which are now sapping and undermining the very foundations of our Republic.

The 1900 NAWSA convention would be Anthony's last; there, she appointed Carrie Chapman Catt as her successor. Catt had worked with Anthony doing fundraising and organizational tasks that led to gaining the vote for women in Colorado. Anthony still maintained her practicality and efficiency when she came into the church where the ceremony was to be held and saw palm trees lining the front of the stage. She said they would have to be removed: "Of course, palms are very fine; I admire them; but I cannot talk to an audience over the tops of a lot of trees."[8]

Once the convention began, the NAWSA delegates felt honored to be in Anthony's presence, knowing how much she had done for the organization. Reports of the event state that "the women went wild as Miss Anthony, erect and alert, with her snowy white hair banded smoothly about her face, walked to the front of the platform, holding the hand of her young co-worker [Catt], of whom she is extremely fond and of whom she expects great things."[9]

Anthony was touched by the support she felt in the room. She told the delegates, "Good friends, I have been reviled most of my life; I have been scoffed and jeered at; I have heard myself called dreadful names and have been the target for every kind of discourtesy—but tonight I am ready to believe that there are people who love and respect me. I am indeed grateful."[10]

SAYING GOOD-BYE TO A FRIEND

In June 1902, Anthony visited her good friend, Stanton, who was no longer in good health, although her mind was still alert. The longtime friends had a good visit, and when they parted, Anthony promised to return for Stanton's eighty-seventh birthday that November. Anthony never got a chance. She received a postcard from Stanton's daughter, Harriot, in October saying that her mother had passed away. Anthony was forced to say good-bye to her dearest lifelong friend. Just months earlier, Anthony had written a letter to Stanton, saying:

> We little dreamed when we began this contest, optimistic with the hope and buoyancy of youth, that half a century later we would be compelled to leave the finish of the battle to another generation of women. But our hearts are filled with joy to know that they enter upon this task equipped with a college education, with business experience, with the fully admitted right to speak in public—all of which were denied to women fifty years ago. They have practically but one point to gain—the suffrage; we had all. These strong, courageous, capable young women will take our place and complete our work. There is an army of them where we were but a handful. Ancient prejudice has become so softened, public sentiment so liberalized and women have so thoroughly demonstrated their ability as to leave not a shadow of doubt that they will carry our cause to victory.[11]

Anthony took a train to New York City the day after hearing the news to help prepare for and attend the funeral. Once in Stanton's apartment, Anthony wrote to a friend, "It is an awful hush ... it seems impossible—that the voice is hushed that I longed to hear for fifty years—longed to hear her opinion of things—before I knew exactly where I stood—It is all at sea—but the laws of nature are still going on. ... What a world it is—it goes right on and on—no matter who lives or who dies!!"[12]

Anthony returned to her home in Rochester, where she still lived with her sister Mary—now her only living sibling.

"A LONG GALAXY OF GREAT WOMEN"

In 1902, Anthony appeared before the Senate Select Committee on Woman Suffrage for the last time. She was the only surviving woman who had petitioned the Senate in 1869. She asked the committee just how long women would have to wait until they would finally be recognized as equal citizens of the United States. It seems they would have to wait a bit longer.

In January 1906, Anthony traveled to Baltimore to take part in the annual National American Woman Suffrage Association convention. Anna Howard Shaw was now president; Catt had stepped down when her husband had taken ill. Anthony felt proud to watch the younger generation of women taking charge and rallying support and vitality into the women's movement.

On February 15, 1906, Anthony attended her eighty-sixth birthday celebration. Hundreds of people sent Anthony well wishes, including President Theodore Roosevelt. Yet Anthony did not want well wishes, she wanted action. Of Roosevelt's words, Anthony said, "I wish the men would do something besides extend congratulations. I have asked President Roosevelt to push the matter of a constitutional amendment allowing suffrage to women by a recommendation to Congress. I would rather have him say a word to Congress for the cause than to praise me endlessly."[13]

After numerous speeches and introductions, Anthony was helped to the podium at her birthday celebration. The audience kept the applause going for 10 full minutes. When they finally grew quiet, Anthony gave what would become her final public speech entitled, "Failure Is Impossible." She ended by saying, "I have met and known most of the progressive women who came after [Mary Wollstonecraft]—Lucretia Mott, the Grimké sisters, Elizabeth Cady Stanton, Lucy Stone—a long galaxy of great women. ... There have been others also just as true and devoted to the cause—I

This portrait of Susan B. Anthony was taken around 1900, the year she stepped down as the president of the National American Woman Suffrage Association. At 80, she remained active in the fight for women's rights. "I want to see you all at work, while I am alive," Anthony said, "so I can scold if you do not do it well."

wish I could name every one—but with such women consecrating their lives, failure is impossible!"[14]

Anthony returned to her home in Rochester, New York, weak and ill. Her sister Mary and a nurse looked after her. Anthony's good friend, Anna Howard Shaw, also came to be with her. During one of their visits, Anthony told Shaw, "I have been striving for over 60 years for a little bit of justice no bigger than that, and yet I must die without obtaining it. ... It seems so cruel."[15] Knowing the end was drawing near, Anthony also offered Shaw some final advice: "No matter what is done or is not done, how you are criticized or misunderstood, or what efforts are made to block your path, remember that the only fear you need have is the fear of not standing by the thing you believe to be right. Take your stand and hold it: then let come what will, and receive the blows like a good soldier."[16]

On March 13, 1906, Susan B. Anthony suffered heart failure after contracting pneumonia. She died in her home on Madison Street in Rochester, New York. Anthony was 86 years old. She is buried in Rochester at Mount Hope Cemetery.

Anthony's funeral drew 10,000 mourners. Numerous eulogies were spoken at Anthony's funeral. The speakers included William Lloyd Garrison, Jr., Carrie Chapman Catt, and Anna Howard Shaw. Shaw's words made an impression on every mourner:

[Susan B. Anthony's] quenchless passion for her cause was that it was yours and mine, the cause of the whole world. She knew that where freedom is, there is the center of power. In it she saw potentially all that humanity might attain when possessed by its spirit. Hence her cause, perfect equality of rights, of opportunity, of privilege for all, civil and political—was to her the bedrock upon which all true progress must rest. Therefore she was nothing, her cause was everything. She knew no existence apart from it. In it she lived and moved and had her being. It was the first and last thought of each day. ... She was truly great: great in her humility and utter lack of pretension.[17]

A newspaper article described the scene of Anthony's funeral as mourners made their way past Anthony's coffin, draped with the American flag: "Rochester made no secret of its personal grief. There must have been people of every creed, political party, nationality, and plane of life in those lines that kept filing through the aisles of Central Church. The youth and age of the land were represented. Every type was there to bow in reverence, respect and grief. Professional men, working men, financiers came to offer homage. Women brought little children to see the face of her who had aimed at being the emancipator of her sex, but whose work had ended just as victory seemed within reach."[18] Above Anthony's head a silk suffrage flag flew with its four gold stars, which represented the four states where women had the right to vote.

Before her death, Anthony had told a family member, "When it *is* a funeral, remember that there should be no tears. Pass on, and go on with the work."[19]

A Life Gone, but Not Forgotten

Susan B. Anthony's strength, dedication, and unwilling-ness to give up helped shape the future lives of women. When Anthony told the world that failure is impossible, it was because she knew—if not in her lifetime—that the women of America were not going to stand back and allow men to make decisions for them. In 1906, Clara Barton, the organizer of the American Red Cross, relayed this story:

A few days ago someone said to me that every woman should stand with bared head before Susan B. Anthony. 'Yes,' I answered, 'and every man as well.' I would not retract these words. I believe that man has benefited by her work as much as woman. For ages he has been trying to carry the burden of life's responsibilities alone and when he has the efficient help of woman he will be grateful. Just now it is new and strange and men cannot comprehend what it would mean, but the change is not far away. The nation is soon to have woman suffrage, and it will be a glad and proud day when it comes.[1]

Fourteen years after the death and 100 years after the birth of Susan B. Anthony, Anthony's lifelong dream was met in 1920: On August 18, the states had ratified the Nineteenth Amendment to the U.S. Constitution, granting the right to vote to all U.S. women over 21. It became nicknamed the "Susan B. Anthony Amendment." The journey to the Nineteenth Amendment had not been an easy one. Anthony's successor, Carrie Chapman Catt, said, "To get the word 'male' in effect out of the Constitution cost the women of the country fifty-two years of pauseless campaign. ... During that time they were forced to conduct 56 campaigns of referenda to male voters, 480 campaigns to get Legislatures to submit suffrage amendments to voters, 47 campaigns to get state constitutional conventions to write woman suffrage into state constitutions; 277 campaigns to get State party conventions to include woman suffrage planks, 30 campaigns to get presidential party campaigns to include woman suffrage planks in party platforms and 19 campaigns with 19 successive Congresses."[2] And yet, at long last, November 1920 brought some 26 million American women the right to vote in an election.

While Anthony is best known for her work toward women's suffrage, we must not forget her other works. She pushed for the emancipation of slaves. She helped get laws passed to improve the rights of married women—allowing them to own property, keep their wages, and share custody of their children. And Anthony worked tirelessly for coeducation.

At a polling place at 111th Street and Broadway in New York City, women lined up on November 2, 1920, to cast their votes for the first time. The Nineteenth Amendment, which gave women the right to vote, was ratified 14 years after the death of Susan B. Anthony.

STAMPS AND COINS

Susan B. Anthony has appeared on two postage stamps—the three-cent in 1936 and the fifty-cent in 1955. She was also the first woman to be honored by having her picture on the dollar coin in 1979. In 1945, the home that Anthony had lived in with her sister Mary on Madison Street in Rochester was purchased in order to create a museum. Artifacts were collected and placed in the house as they appeared when Anthony was alive. In 1966, the Susan B. Anthony House became a National Historic Landmark. In 2004, restoration of the house began, including repairs to the exterior walls and the installation of new heating and cooling systems. And in 2005, work began to return the interior to its original appearance.

The United States gave honor to women's suffrage with a marble statue of Elizabeth Cady Stanton, Susan B. Anthony, and Lucretia Mott in 1921. Adelaide Johnson sculpted the statue. Called *The Portrait Monument*, it is located in Washington, D.C. and is estimated to weigh 26,000 pounds (11,793 kilograms), including its bases.

Many organizations throughout the country continue to work for women's rights. A small handful of them include

IN HER OWN WORDS

At the 1894 annual convention of the National American Woman Suffrage Association, Susan B. Anthony stood before the delegates wearing a black silk dress. Looking into the audience, according to Lynn Sherr's *Failure Is Impossible*, Anthony told them:

> We shall some day be heeded, and when we shall have our amendment to the Constitution of the United States, everybody will think it was always so, just exactly as many young people believe that all the privileges, all the freedom, all the enjoyments which woman now possesses always were hers. They have no idea of how every single inch of ground that she stands upon today has been gained by the hard work of some little handful of women of the past.

the League of Women Voters, which was formed in 1920. Its mission statement reads, "The League of Women Voters, a nonpartisan political organization, encourages informed and active participation in government, works to increase understanding of major public policy issues, and influences public policy through education and advocacy."[3] The National Organization for Women (NOW) was formed in 1966. "The purpose of NOW is to take action to bring women into full participation in the mainstream of American society now, exercising all the privileges and responsibilities thereof in truly equal partnership with men."[4] The Association for Women's Rights in Development (AWID) was formed in 1982. Its mission statement reads, "AWID's mission is to strengthen the voice, impact, and influence of women's rights advocates, organizations, and movements internationally to effectively advance the rights of women."[5]

Susan B. Anthony's lifelong commitment to enriching and bettering women's lives can still be felt today. Each time a woman enters a polling booth, she can be thankful for Anthony's persistence in helping to get her there. Anthony played a key role in helping women to see themselves as equal partners to men. She helped women all over the world believe that failure is impossible.

CHRONOLOGY

1820   Born on February 15 in Adams, Massachusetts.

1837   Goes to school for one term at Deborah Moulson's Female Seminary.

1849   Makes her first public speech at a Daughters of Temperance supper.

1851   Meets Elizabeth Cady Stanton.

1852   The Bloomer becomes a popular new look for women's rights activists; Anthony organizes the Women's State Temperance Society; she attends her first Woman's Rights Convention in September.

1856   Becomes a New York state agent for the American Anti-Slavery Society.

1861   Conducts an anti-slavery campaign with the motto, "No Compromise with Slaveholders. Immediate and Unconditional Emancipation."

1863   Organizes, along with Stanton, the Women's National Loyal League.

1865   The Thirteenth Amendment to the U.S. Constitution is ratified, abolishing slavery.

1866   Anthony helps to establish the American Equal Rights Association (AERA), along with Stanton, Lucretia Mott, and Lucy Stone.

1868   Anthony's newspaper, *The Revolution*, debuts on January 8; the Fourteenth Amendment to the U.S. Constitution is ratified, granting former slaves citizenship and male citizens over the age of 21 the right to vote.

1869   Anthony organizes the first Woman Suffrage Convention in Washington, D.C.; the women's rights movement splits into two groups, with Anthony heading the National Woman Suffrage Association.

1870   The Fifteenth Amendment to the U.S. Constitution is ratified, ensuring a person's race, color, or prior history as a slave cannot be used to keep that person from voting.

1872   Anthony is arrested for voting in a presidential election in November.

1873   Is found guilty of voting in the 1872 election; is fined $100, which Anthony never pays.

1874   In *Minor v. Happersett*, the U.S. Supreme Court decides that citizenship alone does not grant women the right to vote and that each individual state can decide if a woman has the right to vote.

1876   Anthony attends the Centennial Exhibition in Philadelphia.

1881–1902   Anthony, Stanton, and Matilda Joslyn Gage write and publish a four-volume set of books entitled *History of Woman Suffrage*.

1888   Anthony founds the International Council of Women.

1890   Anthony helps found the National American Woman Suffrage Association (NAWSA), the merger of the National Woman Suffrage Association and American Woman Suffrage Association.

1897   Anthony begins work on her biography with Ida Husted Harper.

1902 Anthony's lifelong friend, Elizabeth Cady Stanton, dies.

1902 Anthony appears before the Senate Select Committee on Woman Suffrage for the last time.

1906 Anthony makes her final public speech at her eighty-sixth birthday celebration; Susan B. Anthony dies in her home from heart failure on March 13.

1920 The Nineteenth Amendment to the U.S. Constitution is ratified, allowing women to vote.

NOTES

CHAPTER 1: ARRESTED FOR VOTING

1. "Address of Susan B. Anthony." Available online at http://www.law.umkc.edu/faculty/projects/ftrials/ anthony/anthonyaddress.html.
2. James Daley, editor, *Great Speeches by American Women*. Mineola, N.Y.: Dover Publications, 2008, p. 14.
3. Lynn Sherr, *Failure Is Impossible: Susan B. Anthony in Her Own Words*. New York: Random House, 1995, p. 115.
4. Ibid., p. 116.
5. Ibid., p. 116.

CHAPTER 2: A QUAKER UPBRINGING

1. Kathleen Barry, *Susan B. Anthony: A Biography of a Singular Feminist*. New York: Ballantine Books, 1988, p. 8.
2. Ibid., p. 9.
3. Geoffrey C. Ward and Ken Burns, *Not for Ourselves Alone: The Story of Elizabeth Cady Stanton and Susan B. Anthony*. New York: Alfred A. Knopf, 1999, p. 24.
4. Barry, *A Biography of a Singular Feminist*, p. 11.
5. Sherr, *Failure Is Impossible*, p. 207.
6. Doug Linder, "Susan B. Anthony: A Biography." Available online at http://www.law.umkc.edu/faculty/ projects/ftrials/anthony/sbabiog.html.
7. Sherr, *Failure Is Impossible*, p. 13.
8. Ward and Burns, *Not for Ourselves Alone*, p. 39.
9. Ibid., p. 42.

CHAPTER 3: THE POWER OF REFORM

1. Barry, *A Biography of a Singular Feminist*, p. 59.
2. Ward and Burns, *Not for Ourselves Alone*, p. 47.
3. Sherr, *Failure Is Impossible*, p. 48.

4. Sara M. Evans, *Born for Liberty: A History of Women in America.* New York: The Free Press, 1989, p. 103.
5. Barry, *A Biography of a Singular Feminist*, pp. 64–65.
6. Ward and Burns, *Not for Ourselves Alone*, p. 65.
7. Sherr, *Failure Is Impossible*, p. 14.
8. "Elizabeth Smith Miller." New York History Net. Available online at http://www.nyhistory.com/gerritsmith/esm.htm.
9. Ibid.
10. Sherr, *Failure Is Impossible*, p. 194.
11. Ibid., p. 194.
12. Barry, *A Biography of a Singular Feminist*, p. 68.
13. Ward and Burns, *Not for Ourselves Alone*, p. 67.
14. Sherr, *Failure Is Impossible*, pp. 249–250.
15. Ward and Burns, *Not for Ourselves Alone*, p. 67.
16. Ibid., p. 69.
17. Sherr, *Failure Is Impossible*, p. 19.
18. Ward and Burns, *Not for Ourselves Alone*, p. 73.
19. Ibid., p. 80.
20. Barry, *A Biography of a Singular Feminist*, p. 111.

CHAPTER 4: BREAKING DOWN FENCES
1. Sherr, *Failure Is Impossible*, p. 63.
2. Ibid., p. 170.
3. Ibid., p. 7.
4. Barry, *A Biography of a Singular Feminist*, p. 83.
5. Sherr, *Failure Is Impossible*, p. 55.
6. Ibid., p. 23.
7. Ward and Burns, *Not for Ourselves Alone*, p. 88.
8. Barry, *A Biography of a Singular Feminist*, p. 112.
9. Sherr, *Failure Is Impossible*, p. 297.
10. Barry, *A Biography of a Singular Feminist*, p. 135.
11. Ward and Burns, *Not for Ourselves Alone*, p. 92.
12. Ibid., p. 92.

13. Barry, *A Biography of a Singular Feminist*, p. 147.
14. Ibid., p. 148.

CHAPTER 5: THE AMERICAN CIVIL WAR AND ITS AFTERMATH

1. Barry, *A Biography of a Singular Feminist*, p. 149.
2. Ibid., p. 151.
3. Sherr, *Failure Is Impossible*, p. 34.
4. Ward and Burns, *Not for Ourselves Alone*, p. 101.
5. Ibid., pp. 103–104.
6. Ibid., p. 103.
7. Ibid., p. 104.
8. Barry, *A Biography of a Singular Feminist*, p. 172.
9. Ibid., p. 173.
10. Ibid., p. 176.
11. Ibid., pp. 176–177.
12. Ward and Burns, *Not for Ourselves Alone*, p. 110.
13. Ibid., p. 112.
14. Barry, *A Biography of a Singular Feminist*, p. 223.
15. Ibid., p. 212.
16. Ward and Burns, *Not for Ourselves Alone*, p. 120.
17. Ibid., p. 120.
18. Ibid., pp. 122–123.

CHAPTER 6: A TOWER OF STRENGTH

1. Sherr, *Failure Is Impossible*, p. 121.
2. Ibid., p. 132.
3. Ibid., pp. 122–123.
4. Ibid., p. 81.
5. Ibid., p. xvi.
6. Barry, *A Biography of a Singular Feminist*, p. 218.
7. Ibid., pp. 218–219.
8. Ward and Burns, *Not for Ourselves Alone*, p. 134.
9. Barry, *A Biography of a Singular Feminist*, pp. 232–233.

10. Sherr, *Failure Is Impossible*, p. 127.
11. Ward and Burns, *Not for Ourselves Alone*, p. 141.
12. Ibid., p. 143.
13. Ibid., p. 144.
14. Ibid., p. 144.
15. Ibid., p. 145.
16. Ibid., p. 149.
17. Ibid., p. 150.
18. Ibid., p. 150.
19. Ibid., p. 152.
20. Ibid., p. 154.
21. Ibid., p. 154.
22. "The Trial of Susan B. Anthony—A 100-Year Chronology." Available online at http://www.law.umkc.edu/faculty/projects/ftrials/anthony/timeline.html.
23. Daley, *Great Speeches by American Women*, pp. 13–14.
24. Ibid., p. 20.
25. Evans, *A History of Women in America*, p. 153.
26. Ward and Burns, *Not for Ourselves Alone*, p. 179.
27. Ibid., p. 183.
28. Ibid., p. 183.

CHAPTER 7: A NEW GENERATION OF WOMEN
1. Sherr, *Failure Is Impossible*, p. 126.
2. Ibid., p. 329.
3. Barry, *A Biography of a Singular Feminist*, p. 334.
4. Ibid., pp. 292–293.
5. Ward and Burns, *Not for Ourselves Alone*, p. 204.
6. Ibid., p. 204.
7. Sherr, *Failure Is Impossible*, p. 319.
8. Ibid., p. 320.
9. Ibid., p. 320.
10. Ibid., p. 321.
11. Ward and Burns, *Not for Ourselves Alone*, p. 207.

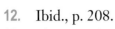

12. Ibid., p. 208.

13. Sherr, *Failure Is Impossible*, p. 324.

14. Ward and Burns, *Not for Ourselves Alone*, p. 212.

15. Ibid., p. 212.

16. Barry, *A Biography of a Singular Feminist*, p. 355.

17. Sherr, *Failure Is Impossible*, p. 326.

18. Ibid., p. 325.

19. Linder, "Susan B. Anthony: A Biography."

CHAPTER 8: A LIFE GONE, BUT NOT FORGOTTEN

1. Sherr, *Failure Is Impossible*, p. 315.

2. Gail Collins, *America's Women: 400 Years of Dolls, Drudges, Helpmates, and Heroines*. New York: HarperCollins, 2003, p. 307.

3. "The League of Women Voters: About Us." League of Women Voters Web site. Available online at http://www.lwv.org/AM/Template.cfm?Section=About_Us.

4. "The National Organization for Women's 1966 Statement of Purpose." National Organization for Women Web site. Available online at http://www.now.org/history/purpos66.html.

5. "What Is AWID?" Association for Women's Rights in Development Web site. Available online at http://www.awid.org/About-AWID/What-is-AWID.

BIBLIOGRAPHY

Barry, Kathleen. *Susan B. Anthony: A Biography of a Singular Feminist*. New York: Ballantine Books, 1988.

Collins, Gail. *America's Women: 400 Years of Dolls, Drudges, Helpmates, and Heroines*. New York: HarperCollins, 2003.

Daley, James, editor. *Great Speeches by American Women*. Mineola, N.Y.: Dover Publications, 2008.

Evans, Sara M. *Born for Liberty: A History of Women in America*. New York: The Free Press, 1989.

Linder, Doug. "Famous American Trials: The Trial of Susan B. Anthony," 2001. Available online at http://www.law.umkc.edu/faculty/projects/ftrials/anthony/sbahome.html.

Sherr, Lynn. *Failure Is Impossible: Susan B. Anthony in Her Own Words*. New York: Random House, 1995.

Ward, Geoffrey C. and Ken Burns. *Not for Ourselves Alone: The Story of Elizabeth Cady Stanton and Susan B. Anthony*. New York: Alfred A. Knopf, 1999.

FURTHER RESOURCES

BOOKS

Ching, Jacqueline and Juliet Ching. *Individual Freedom, Civic Responsibility: Women's Rights*. New York: Rosen Publishing Group, 2001.

Monroe, Judy. *The Susan B. Anthony Women's Voting Rights Trial: A Headline Court Case*. Berkeley Heights, N.J.: Enslow Publishers, 2002.

Mountjoy, Shane. *The Women's Rights Movement: Moving Toward Equality*. New York: Chelsea House Publishers, 2007.

Sigerman, Harriet. *Laborers for Liberty: American Women 1865–1890*, New York: Oxford University Press, 1994.

WEB SITES

Association for Women's Rights in Development
http://www.awid.org

The Elizabeth Cady Stanton and Susan B. Anthony Papers Project (Rutgers University)
http://ecssba.rutgers.edu

League of Women Voters
http://www.lwv.org

National Organization for Women
http://www.now.org

National Women's History Project
http://www.nwhp.org

Susan B. Anthony House
http://www.susanbanthonyhouse.org

Women's Rights National Historical Park
http://www.nps.gov/wori/

PICTURE CREDITS

PAGE

10: © Corbis
18: Getty Images
22: AP Images
28: AP Images
34: Library of Congress, Prints and Photographs Division, LC-USZ62-970
41: © The Metropolitan Museum of Art / Art Resource, N.Y.
45: © Corbis
53: © Corbis
58: AP Images
61: Library of Congress, Prints and Photographs Division, LC-USZ6-2055

66: Library of Congress, Prints and Photographs Division, LC-USZ62-127495
71: Getty Images
77: The Granger Collection, New York
80: © Bettmann/Corbis
85: © Bettmann/Corbis
90: © Bettmann/Corbis
95: Getty Images
100: © Corbis
105: © Corbis
110: © Bettmann/Corbis

INDEX

A

abolitionism
  leaders, 18, 27–30, 33, 40, 42, 43, 48, 52–54, 55, 59
  lectures, 30, 52–54
  meetings, 21, 27, 29
Adams, Massachusetts, 13
African American
  equality, 63
  voting rights, 63–65, 67–68
  women, 64–65
American Anti-Slavery Society, 40, 42, 48, 55–57, 63
American Civil War, 55–62
American Equal Rights Association (AERA)
  meetings, 64–65, 69–70
American Red Cross, 108
American Woman Suffrage Association (AWSA), 71, 88, 91
Anthony, Ann Eliza (sister), 15
Anthony, Daniel (father), 13, 23
  abolitionism, 27
  bankruptcy, 17, 20
  death, 29, 61–63, 88
  farm, 20, 25, 26, 57
  scandal, 14–15
  work of, 14–17, 19
Anthony, Daniel (brother), 28, 47, 62, 82, 83
  childhood, 15
  newspaper, 63, 83
Anthony, Guelma (sister), 8, 75, 82
  childhood, 15, 17
  death, 87–88
  marriage, 19–20
  voting, 78–79
Anthony, Hannah (sister), 8, 75, 82
  childhood, 15
  death, 87–88
  marriage, 20
  voting, 78–79
Anthony, J. Merritt (brother), 28
  childhood, 15
Anthony, Lucy Read (mother), 19, 23, 75
  abolitionism, 27
  death, 87
  farm, 20, 25, 26, 57
  scandal, 14–15
Anthony, Mary (sister), 8, 23, 26, 98
  childhood, 15
  living with, 82, 94, 103, 105, 110
  voting, 78–79
Anthony, Susan B.
  birth, 13
  childhood, 13–17
  chronology, 113–115
  coins and stamps, 110
  death, 106–107
  education, 17–19
  illnesses and ailments, 15–16, 46, 98, 105
  and marriage, 21, 44, 82
  public speaking, 11, 23–24, 27, 39–40, 44, 46–49, 52, 57–58, 67–68, 73–74, 76, 79, 82, 84, 86–87, 89–91, 96–97, 99, 102, 104
  teaching, 19–20, 23–24
arrest and trial
  fine, 12, 81
  injustice of, 11
  verdict, 11, 79
  for voting, 7–8, 79, 81
Association for Women's Rights in Development (AWID), 112
Auld, Hugh, 29
Avery, Rachel Foster, 94

B

Barry, Kathleen, 14, 46
Barton, Clara, 108
Battenville, New York, 16–17
Beecher, Henry Ward, 71
Blackwell, Alice Stone, 91
Blackwell, Henry, 44, 60, 67
Bloomer, Amelia, 30
  The Bloomer, 33, 35
  The Lily, 30, 33, 35
Bly, Nellie, 19, 62
Born for Liberty: A History of Women in America (Evans), 31, 91
Brown, Antoinette, 37, 44, 50
Brown, Olympia, 68

Bullard, Laura Curtis, 72
Burns, Ken
    on Anthony, 16, 22, 26, 59

C

Cady, Daniel, 50
Cady, Eleazar, 50
Caldwell, Joseph, 24
Caldwell, Margaret, 20, 24–25
Canajoharie Academy, 20, 23–24
Catt, Carrie Chapman, 102, 104,
    106, 109
Centennial Exhibition, 81, 83–84
Center Falls, New York, 19
Collins, Gail, 96
Colorado
    women's right to vote in, 97, 102
Constitution, United States, 92, 111
    Fifteenth Amendment, 69–71, 76
    Fourteenth Amendment, 8, 9, 11,
        63–65, 70, 76, 78
    Nineteenth Amendment, 109
    Sixteenth Amendment, 70, 75, 86
    steps toward an amendment, 9,
        59, 63, 81, 88, 91, 104
    Thirteenth Amendment, 61
Covey, Edward, 29
Curtis, George William, 65, 67

D

Daughters of Temperance, 23–24, 26
Davies, Charles, 47
Deborah Moulson's Female Semi-
    nary, 17–19
Declaration of Rights for Women,
    81, 83–84
Douglass, Frederick, 62
    abolitionism, 27, 29, 52, 63
Dred Scott decision, 48

E

Emancipation Proclamation, 59
Eunice Kenyon's Friends' Seminary,
    19–20
Evans, Sara
    Born for Liberty: A History of
        Women in America, 31, 91

F

Failure Is Impossible (Sherr), 24, 62,
    87, 101, 111
Ferry, Thomas, 83
Foster, Abby, 30
Foster, Stephen, 30, 52

G

Gage, Matilda Joslyn, 81, 84
Garrison, William Lloyd,
    work of, 27, 29–31, 50–52, 55,
        57, 63
Garrison, William Lloyd, Jr., 106
Gates, New York, 20, 25
Grant, Ulysses S., 8
Greeley, Horace, 31, 65, 67
Grimké sisters, 104

H

Happersett, Reese, 81
Harper, Frances, 64
Harper, Ida Husted, 100
Harvard University, 97
Hawley, Joseph Roswell, 83
Hill, David J., 97
History of Woman Suffrage, 84
Hooker, Isabella Beecher, 72
Hunt, Ward (judge), 11–12, 79, 81

I

Idaho
    women's right to vote in, 97
International Council of Women,
    89, 94
"Is It a Crime for a Citizen of the
    United States to Vote" (speech), 7,
    11, 79, 81

J

Jenkins, Theresa, 93
Johnson, Adelaide, 111

L

League of Women Voters, 112
Lee, Richard Henry, 83
Life and Work of Susan B. Anthony: A
    Story of the Evolution of the Status of
    Women, The, 100

Lincoln, Abraham, 62
 inaugural address, 55
 and slavery, 55, 57, 59

M

Married Woman's Property Act
 children, 32–33, 49, 57
 earned money, 27, 32, 39, 49
 inheritance, 27, 39
 property, 49
May, Samuel, 40, 53–54, 62
McLean, Aaron, 19
McLean, John, 16, 19
Miller, Elizabeth Smith, 33
Minor, Virginia, 81
Mosher, Eugene, 20
Mott, Lucretia, 68, 111
 work of, 18, 21, 52, 64, 104
Mott, Lydia, 18

N

National American Woman Suf-
 frage Association (NAWSA)
 conventions, 102, 104, 111
 members, 91–92, 98–99, 101–
  102
National Archives, 9
National Organization for Women
 (NOW), 112
National Woman's Rights Conven-
 tion, 49–52, 56, 64
National Woman Suffrage Associa-
 tion (NWSA), 70, 78, 83, 88
 convention, 74, 76, 86
"Negro's Hour," 63
New England Woman Suffrage
 Association, 70–71
New Rochelle, New York, 19
New York Constitution, 8, 65, 96
New York legislature, 39, 49, 57
New York State Teachers Conven-
 tion, 39, 47–48
North Star (publication), 29

O

"On Behalf of the Woman Suffrage
 Amendment" (speech), 86–87,
 89–91

P

Panic of 1837, 17, 20
People's Party, 78
Perkins, Mary, 17
Philadelphia Female Anti-Slavery
 Society, 21
Phillips, Wendell
 work of, 50–52, 63–64
Portrait Monument, The, 111
Purvis, Hattie, 64

Q

Quaker
 abolitionists, 18, 27, 29–30
 beliefs and ideals, 13–15
 schools, 17, 19
 upbringing, 13, 15, 32, 47

R

Revolution, The (newspaper), 68–69,
 71–72, 75
Rochester, New York, 20, 23
 conventions in, 35, 37
 elections in, 8, 78–79
 home in, 8, 29, 79, 82, 94, 100,
  103, 105–106, 110–111
Rochester, University of
 women admitted to, 97–98
Roosevelt, Theodore, 104
Rose, Ernestine, 37, 39

S

Sargent, Arlen A., 86
Selden, Henry, 79
Senate Select Committee on Woman
 Suffrage, 104
Seneca Falls, New York, 30, 49
Seneca Falls Woman's Rights Con-
 vention, 21–23
 Declaration of Sentiments, 22
Sewall, May Wright, 94
Shaw, Anna Howard, 104–106
Sherr, Lynn
 Failure Is Impossible, 24, 62, 87,
  101, 111
Slavery, 39, 48
 anti-slavery movement, 27–30, 40,
  42, 43, 52–54, 55–56, 59–60

and Civil War, 57–59
freedom and rights, 59–61, 63,
  109
Smith, Gerrit, 33, 52, 63
Sons of Temperance, 32
Stanton, Elizabeth Cady, 22, 111
  death, 102–103
  family, 31, 44, 50–51, 76, 84, 86,
    88, 94, 102
  friendship with, 31–32, 51–52,
    84, 102
  illness, 75, 77, 102
  The Woman's Bible, 98–99
  work of, 21, 23, 30–31, 33, 36–38,
    39, 49–52, 59, 63–65, 67–71,
    77, 81, 83–84, 86, 89, 91–92,
    94, 104
Stanton, Harriot, 86, 102
Stanton, Henry, 31, 50–51, 76
Stanton, Margaret, 84, 94
Stanton, Robert, 94
Stanton, Theodore, 86, 88
State Woman's Rights Convention,
  39
Stone, Lucy, 33
  family, 44, 60, 91
  work of, 31, 37, 59, 60, 64, 67–68,
    70–72, 88–89, 91–92, 104
Stowe, Harriet Beecher, 72
Sumner, Charles, 60
Susan B. Anthony House, 110–111
Syracuse, New York, 30, 53–54
Syracuse University, 97

T

Thompson, George, 29–31
Tilton, Theodore, 72
Tubman, Harriet, 56
Train, George Francis
  support of, 67–68, 72
Truth, Sojourner, 65

U

Underground Railroad, 27, 56
United States
  citizens, 7–8, 11–12, 79, 81, 86,
    104
  government, 7–8, 9, 59, 63–65,

69–70, 75, 76, 79, 81, 86, 88,
  104, 109
  Supreme Court, 48, 79, 81
Utah
  women's right to vote in, 97

V

voting
  registering, 8, 78, 81
  right to, 7–8, 11–12, 32, 39, 43,
    45, 50, 63, 65, 67–70, 74, 75,
    76, 78–79, 81, 86, 88–91, 93–94,
    96, 97, 101, 104, 109, 112

W

Ward, Geoffrey
  on Anthony, 16, 22, 26, 59
Wilkinson, Helen, 97
"Winter of the Mobs, The," 52–54
Wollstonecraft, Mary, 68, 104
Woman's Bible, The (Stanton), 98–99
Woman's Journal, The, 71–72
Women's National Loyal League, 59
women's rights, 42
  articles on, 30
  children, 32–33, 49, 57
  conventions, 21–23, 37, 49–52,
    56, 60, 64, 74, 76, 86, 102, 104
  divorce, 32, 36, 50–52
  education, 31–32, 43, 47–48, 88,
    97–98, 103, 109
  labor, 44, 69–70
  married women, 27, 32–33, 39,
    49, 57
  to vote, 7–8, 11–12, 32, 39, 43,
    45, 50, 63, 65, 67–70, 74, 75,
    76, 78–79, 81, 86, 88–91, 93–94,
    96, 97, 101, 104, 109, 112
Women's State Temperance Society,
  99
  founding of, 32
  work of, 35–38
Woodhull, Victoria, 76, 78
Working Women's Association, 69
World Anti-Slavery Conference, 21
Wright, Martha, 52
Wyoming
  women's right to vote in, 93, 97

ABOUT THE AUTHOR

ANNE M. TODD received a Bachelor of Arts degree in English and American Indian studies from the University of Minnesota. She has written more than 20 nonfiction children's books, including biographies on American Indians, political leaders, and entertainers. Todd is the author of the following Chelsea House books: *Roger Maris*, from the BASEBALL SUPERSTARS series; *Mohandas Gandhi*, from the SPIRITUAL LEADERS AND THINKERS series; *Chris Rock* and *Jamie Foxx*, both from the BLACK AMERICANS OF ACHIEVEMENT, LEGACY EDITION series; and *Vera Wang*, from the ASIAN AMERICANS OF ACHIEVEMENT series. She lives in Prior Lake, Minnesota, with her husband, Sean, and three sons, Spencer, William, and Henry.